THE
DA VINCI
MOLE

DR. IAN BROWNE

BENBELLA BOOKS, INC. • *Dallas, Texas*

This is a work of fiction. It is, in fact, a parody. All characters and events in this book are fictitious. Any similarities characters bear to copyrighted characters and material, or individuals living or dead, are purely coincidental. In other words, none of this is necessarily true, even if the narrator says it's true, even if we say the word "fact."

Did you really need us to tell you that?

The Da Vinci Mole ©BenBella Books

BenBella Books, Inc.
6440 N. Central Expressway, Suite 617
Dallas, TX 75206
www.benbellabooks.com
send feedback to feedback@benbellabooks.com

Printed in the United States of America

10 9 8 7 6 5 4 3 2 1

Library of Congress Cataloging-in-Publication Data

Browne, Ian.
    The Da Vinci mole / Ian Browne.
        p. cm.
    ISBN 1-932100-90-3
    1. Brown, Dan, 1964—Parodies, imitations, etc. 2. Brown, Dan, 1964– Da Vinci code. I. Title.

    PN6231.P3B77 2006
    813'.54—dc22

                                                                2006003170

Proofreading by Jessica Keet and Stacia Seaman
Cover design by Laura Watkins
Illustrations by Ralph Voltz
Text Design and Composition by John Reinhardt Book Design
Printed by Victor Graphics, Inc.

Distributed by Independent Publishers Group
To order call (800) 888-4741 • www.ipgbook.com

For special sales contact Yara Abuata at yara@benbellabooks.com

To Mimi, my first true love

FACTS

The Church of Scientology—a Church founded in 1954 by L. Ron Hubbard—is a real organization. Scientologists claim that mankind is polluted by the debris of space aliens who died 75 million years ago. This transparently absurd cover story is designed to mask the true nature and objectives of the Scientologists, which are revealed in this book. The links between Scientology, the order of the Masons, UFO sightings, the dollar bill and alien anal probing are all genuine and well documented.

Similarly, the facts revealed on the nature of modern art, the building of the pyramids, Leonardo da Vinci, Jesus and the early Church, Fermi's Paradox, intelligent design, proof of the existence of God, Procter & Gamble, human evolution, and the secret nature of the current White House administration are all quite true, and amply supported by the extensive bibliography.

AUTHOR'S NOTE

This is a work of fiction. Fiction was not my preference, but an exigency I was forced into out of desperation. I have endured every indignity in dealing with the editorial sadists at BenBella (a publishing house, named, quite aptly, for a Muslim terrorist) but I was allowed one concession, this unedited author's note. Through it I must get across to you, my audience, the importance of the present volume, a book that I freely confess looks less important than the latest issue of *MAD* Magazine, and is likely to have a shorter shelf life.

It seems almost hopeless, but I do not despair. I was trained better than that, and, although I now turn on my masters, I still respect their teachings.

My name is not Dr. Ian Browne. This is a pseudonym chosen by my accursed publisher for obvious and base commercial reasons. I cannot reveal my true name to you, for my own safety, but suffice it to say that you would recognize it instantly, and that knowledge of my true identity would help you understand the critical importance of this work.

This book was originally a non-fiction volume. I wrote it with great care. My agent had secured a seven-figure book deal with

Jane Friedman at HarperCollins. I was given carte blanche to tell my story as I saw fit. But certain events convinced me that I could not safely use my real name. When I told Jane that I must use a pseudonym she became furious and tore up our agreement. Surely the importance of this volume is revealed by the seriousness of the content, not the name of the author! My profession is equally frivolous, but I expected more of publishing.

My agent abandoned me, and I shopped this volume around from publisher to publisher, approaching ever-more obscure and insignificant publishers, only to be rejected by them all. Finally, in desperation, I approached something called BenBella Books.

They agreed to publish my volume, but only on the condition that I fictionalize it. In desperation I agreed, only to hear their further demands. The book must be in the form of a parody of *The Da Vinci Code*.

You cannot appreciate the awful irony of this demand. *The Da Vinci Code*, a malicious pyramid of lies, was written to distract the American public from the real truth. And it couldn't have been more successful. As millions debate the truth and falsehood of *The Da Vinci Code*, the real conspiracy goes on, unnoticed. And it dwarfs in importance the feeble conspiracy described in that book.

This is a work of fiction. But the story it tells of mankind, the Church, art and present-day America is very true. This book is based on decades of research[1] as well as the personal access I've had to the private files of the most important secret organization in this country. I've done my homework. I know the history of art and of the Church; I know the history of psychiatry and, I dare say, you don't. I pray that you take this seriously.

---

[1] I refer you to the bibliography, which contains many solid references.

Unlike *The Da Vinci Code*, which suggests that the best course of action is to do nothing at all (which is exactly what they want you to do), at the end of this book your course of action will be crystal clear. I hope you have the courage to take action. I cannot do it alone, and the fate of humanity hangs in the balance.

PROLOGUE

Eric San Leté wove awkwardly as he stumbled through the halls of the Whitney, his breath coming in wheezing gasps. At seventy-three, he was still in fine shape, but his body no longer had the strength it once did. And the creature behind him was tireless. The sterile halls of the Whitney flew past him as he ran. He could barely make out the outlines of the art around him in the amber glow of the dim after-hours lighting.

A Frenchman, San Leté was a distinguished curator at the Louvre, and was spending a sabbatical year at the Whitney. But he already knew the Whitney as one knows a dear friend, and he could picture each unseen painting as he flew past it. The secret meaning of each flashed into his mind as he staggered past it, meanings known only to him and his Masonic brethren.

The footsteps behind him were closer now, and he was too exhausted to run any farther. He turned and saw a man approaching in the dim light.

"Hello, Eric," Karl greeted him. "It doesn't have to be like this. W is prepared to call a truce; there's no reason we need to be in conflict. Just tell me where the WMD[2] is."

---

[2] Weapon of Mental Development.

Eric smiled feebly. "The WMD will be released very soon. Have no fears on that score. You should welcome it."

"It will never be released. Tell me where it is and this can all be over. I can't imagine any weapon you developed could be very impressive. But you know W; he likes to be thorough. So where is it, Eric?"

"Karl, you bastard," San Leté wheezed. "Finding the WMD isn't going to solve anything. Neither will getting rid of me. What you are doing is wrong, and ultimately will fail, as it always has in the past. Why must you dominate? Why can't you just live, appreciate art, enjoy the fruits of this great civilization we live in?" Exhausted by the effort to speak these words, he sank to the floor, breathing heavily.

Karl approached to within fifteen feet of San Leté, pulled up a guard chair and sat. "You want to debate philosophy? Fine. I'm in no rush. But I won't be telling you anything you don't already know. You just can't accept it. God is dead, Eric. We are the aimless products of mindless evolution, and the only meaning is the meaning we make. The will to power. It's the only thing that gives life meaning. If you want to try to look for meaning in art, be my guest. But you got in our way. Not nice."

Eric spat, or tried to in his feeble state. "Spare me the *Nietzsche for Dummies* lecture, Karl. I've heard it before. God is alive and well, and She doesn't like what you are doing. I'm warning you, turn around and leave now."

Karl laughed, removing a strange metal device from his jacket pocket. It was nine inches long and gleamed with a high sheen. "You're warning me? I don't think that's very realistic."

"Look behind you," Eric warned. He smiled triumphantly. Karl turned and saw the painting that Eric had ripped from the wall. Even in the dim light he could see it was some Mondrian-esque monstrosity. "That's right, Karl, I triggered the silent alarm. The police will be here any second. Leave while you can."

Karl laughed again. "Eric, you are a fool. This is New York, not Paris. It'll be hours before the police arrive. And who do you think controls the police in this town anyway?" He got up and walked toward San Leté, holding the strange device in front of him. Eric screamed...

Twenty minutes later Karl Rove emerged from the side entrance to the Whitney. He hummed to himself as he hailed a taxi on his way back to Washington D.C.

Professor Hank Thomas was on top of the world. It was past midnight, and he should have been sleeping, but he couldn't stop thinking of his triumph. His presidential suite at the Four Seasons was filled with flowers and Dom Perignon (he ordered both himself), and he contentedly sipped his drink and smoked his expensive Cuban cigar.

He stood in front of the mirror admiring his reflection. His round, cheerful face held an expression of vague befuddlement that he knew women found intriguing. His receding hairline revealed a broad expanse of scalp, but his mother insisted the bald patch only accentuated his virile appeal. He tended to agree.

His lecture to the Jackson Pollock Admirer's Society had been brilliant, and the room, which normally sat as many as twenty, had been filled to overcapacity. He was greeted by the beautiful secretary of the society, Hadley Boyd, who gave him a warm smile as they shook hands. "A pleasure to meet you, Professor Thomas."

"The pleasure is mine, Ms. Boyd. Am I correct that you will be introducing me?" When she nodded, he added, "Let me take the liberty of giving you this article to read in your introduction. As you can see, *Obscure Symbologists Magazine* named me one of their twenty most interesting people."

"You want me to read this? Out loud?" she asked uncertainly.

"If you would," Hank suggested smoothly. "I think it gives folks a nice introduction to the complexity that is *moi*. And, incidentally, I have nothing scheduled after this lecture. I'd be delighted to take you back to my room and show you some of my most recent, unpublished work." He gave her a seductive smile.

"Umm...that's, um, a great honor, Professor, but unfortunately I'm very busy this evening," Boyd replied uncomfortably.

"Yes, well that's fine," Brown responded weakly. His brilliant symbologist mind then clicked into action, regrettably late. Hadley was, of course, an unusual woman's name. It was the name of Hemingway's first wife, the only wife he truly loved. But his *son* was also named Hadley, a common man's name in the UK. And Hemingway was deathly afraid of lesbians, having had an unfortunate encounter with Gertrude Stein and Alice B. Tolkas. This was not definitive, but consider the last name— Boyd, which breaks up symbolically into boy-d. The letter "d" is derived from the Greek *delta*, meaning change, creating the symbolic meaning "boy-change." *Delta* is derived indirectly from the Aramaic *derka*, meaning similar or like. This generates the symbolic meaning "boy-like." The conclusion was definitive. Hadley Boyd was a lesbian, and if only he had thought this through a little more quickly this awkward situation could have been avoided. He quickly rallied. "I approve of your life choice," he declared magnanimously.

"Uh, thanks," Boyd replied, inching away.

Aside from that awkwardness, the evening had been a stunning success. His description of the hidden meanings in Jackson Pollock was brilliant and he was a big hit. Naturally, he did not reveal the deepest meanings in the works; these were secrets he shared with no one. He sunk into the chair, in the peaceful reverie that only contemplation of one's own great wealth can provide, when the phone rang.

He glanced at his Rolex in irritation. It was almost one A.M. "Hello?"

"Dr. Thomas, I am the concierge. My apologies for calling this late, but an Inspector McGruff is here to see you."

"Please tell him that it's way too late; I'll see him in..." Hank heard a large crack as his hotel door was violently kicked in. The door flung aside and there stood a massive, bull-like man in a rumpled suit and trench coat. Hank lowered the phone slowly.

"Can I help you?" Hank asked tentatively.

"I am Inspector Sean McGruff, known as 'the Poodle'," Mc-Gruff declared in a surprisingly high-pitched voice.

"The Poodle?"

"The miniature poodle is a far more powerful dog than most people realize. It can yap, loudly and consistently, for over twenty-four hours."

"Okay," Hank replied slowly.

"But more to the point. We need your help, monsieur."

Hank didn't know where to start. "You're French? You don't sound French."

"What? Of course I'm not French. I hate the damn French. The French are effeminate, wine-sipping defeatists. I ought to beat the crap out of you for suggesting I'm French. You're the one who is French."

"But you called me monsieur..." Hank replied feebly.

"As a courtesy to you, you damn Frog."

"But I'm not French."

McGruff pulled out his pad and flicked through it. "Let me get this straight. You've devoted your life to studying art?"

"Yes."

"An expert in symbols?"

"Yes."

"And you filled your own room with flowers and French champagne?"

"Well, yes."

"And you aren't French?"

"No! I'm American. Well, Californian."

"Californian. I see," McGruff grunted in satisfaction. "Close enough. Anyway, let's go. Eric San Leté, an important art expert and symbologist, has been murdered."

"San Leté! I was supposed to see him tomorrow. He died tonight?"

McGruff coughed apologetically. "Last night, actually."

Hank stared at him uncomprehendingly.

"This is New York; there's a lot of crime. We don't get to every alarm immediately. Sue me." He paused. "But the important thing is that San Leté left a cryptic message. We have our cryptologists working on it now."

"So that's why you are here. You want me to decipher it?"

McGruff hesitated, then gave a sinister smile, "Uh, yeah, sure, that's it. Now let's get moving."

They drove north on Madison Avenue, a street best known for its infamous association with the nation's leading advertising agencies. But the portion of Madison Avenue north of 60th Street was part of the arts district radiating off of the monumental Metropolitan Museum, and the street was lined with overpriced art galleries, upscale antique shops and overly precious eateries. *I'm an expert on art,* Hank thought.

It wasn't long before they approached the distinctive outlines of the Whitney Museum. The Whitney was a huge, concrete square, or series of squares, that combined made a striking architectural statement. "What do you think of our Whitney, Professor Thomas?" McGruff asked.

Hank knew this was a trick question. "It's quite imposing," he ventured.

"It's a monstrosity and a menace," McGruff declared.

Hank stayed silent.

"It should be torn down. This building has killed three people so far this year."

"Surely that's a bit of an exaggeration," Hank said.

"Really? See those square indentations?" In the darkness,

Hank could barely make out numerous square indentations in the wall, seemingly set at random. "Those are 300-pound blocks of concrete; seven of them broke loose and fell in the last year. The building is a freaking hazard."

Hank saw his point. Still, he felt the need to defend the artistic structure. "Well, you have to consider the entire artistic gestalt in the context of an ever-changing aesthetic dynamic," he muttered.

McGruff glared at him, and hauled him into the building.

Entering the hall, McGruff pulled Hank through a crowd of police. The scene was horrific, as was the smell. Eric San Leté was dead. He lay face down, naked below the waist. In the moments before his death he had carefully arranged his body with his arms and legs outstretched, reminiscent of Da Vinci's famous *Vitruvian Man*.

On the wall he had drawn a rectangle, apparently with his own feces. Within the rectangle there was a seemingly random assortment of curving lines and dots. Below the painting were the initials "SP," then four lines of writing:

> Oh, Rubick's Cube!
>
> Oh, Alien Weapon!
> Find Hank Thomas
> (Ehay idn'tday oday itway)

Finally, below the writing, there was a series of numbers:

> 24 103 17 3 72

"You can see we've got quite a puzzle on our hands," McGruff stated. "This rectangle is meaningless, but he does name you quite specifically. We believe the line below is in some kind

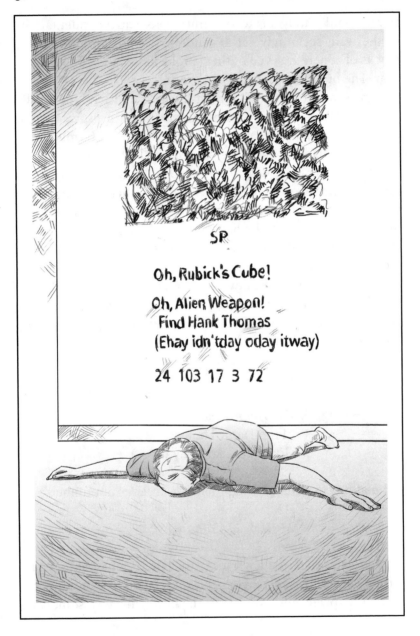

of code. As you know, San Leté was an expert cryptologist. But we have our best men working on it and we'll get it cracked. It's only a matter of time."

"It's pig latin," Hank said. "The last two lines say 'Find Hank Thomas. (He didn't do it.)'"

"Yeah, right, good try, Thomas," McGruff scoffed. "I'll rely on our experts, if it's all the same to you. In the meantime, I need to ask you a few questions."

"Shoot."

"Why were you meeting Eric San Leté tomorrow?"

"I don't know. The meeting was at his request."

"Why would he want to meet you?"

"Well, we were both experts in modern art and cryptology. Maybe he wanted to compare notes."

"And why did you kill him?"

"I didn't kill him!" Pause. "Does that ever work?"

McGruff smiled ruefully. "More often than you'd think, Frenchie."

At that moment a young and very attractive woman pushed her way through the crowd. "I must see the body," she insisted, her eyes filled with tears.

McGruff blocked her path. "Okay, sweetheart, what's your story?"

The young woman explained. "My name is Saphie Paradise. I'm a French citizen, a senior at Harvard University. Your men told me my grandfather had been killed. He raised me since I was a little girl. This message is clearly meant for me. The initials, SP, stand for Princess Saphie, which he called me as a child. He was dyslexic, as I'm sure you know, so clearly he accidentally reversed the letters. In any case he called me yesterday, promising to give me profound revelations about my family and telling me that we were both in danger. But I ignored him, as I cut off ties with him four years ago after catching him in a revolting act that is possibly subject to multiple interpretations now that I think about it."

"Whoa, slow down, young lady," McGruff demanded. "I don't need your life story. I'll take mine with two sugars."

As Saphie glared at McGruff, Hank quietly slipped away. He had already unraveled the message and needed to get to the Jackson Pollock wing as quickly as possible.

Seemingly oblivious, McGruff quietly observed Hank's departure. It was all according to his plan. He wasn't called "the Poodle" for nothing. Yap. Yap.

THREE

Hank stared up at the giant *Autumn Rhythm*. One of Jackson Pollock's great works, it dominated the room, roughly eleven feet tall and seventeen feet wide. Eric San Leté was a true artistic genius. In a two-foot by three-foot rectangle, he had duplicated the Pollock masterpiece. His was much smaller, of course, and monochromatic—there were limits to feces as a medium. Nevertheless, it was an almost perfect replica; there might have been a few differences, if he recalled San Leté's painting exactly, but it was incredibly close, particularly as it had been drawn from memory.

But more to the point. *Why did San Leté want me to come to this painting?* He examined it carefully, looked behind it and all around. He found nothing. He was about to give up in despair when he heard footsteps behind him. He whirled. It was Saphie Paradise.

"You spotted it too," she observed. He looked her over carefully. She was in her early twenties, with shoulder-length black hair and petite Gallic features. He thought he had never seen anyone so lovely.

"Yes, it was quite obvious, at least to a Pollock scholar such as myself. You must have quite an eye for art yourself."

"Well, I was raised by Eric San Leté, a man of great brilliance and gentleness," she said modestly. "He was the kindest, most wonderful parent anyone could have ever had. But that didn't stop me washing my hands of him, despite his numerous and desperate pleas for reconciliation, for the rest of his life, when I found him doing something completely revolting." She paused. "Unless I misinterpreted it," she added weakly.

"That's all water under the bridge now, young lady," Hank soothed.

"So why did my grandfather want to find you? And why send you here?"

"I'll be damned if I know. Do you have any idea why he was killed?"

"As I said, we haven't been close lately. He's recently left a number of messages saying that danger was approaching for both of us and that he had to speak to me. Naturally I assumed that he was making this all up to scare me into seeing him," Saphie explained. "I might have been wrong about that."

"Well, we're dead-ended here. I've searched everywhere, but couldn't find a thing," Hank said.

"Have you tried this?" Saphie held up an ultraviolet light.

"Now where did you get one of those?"

"Oh, it's the biggest thing at Harvard these days, at our sex parties." She blushed prettily. "It's not even considered a proper orgy anymore if you don't have black light."

"Okay," Hank said slowly. He was enormously attracted to Saphie, but he had already decided she was a lesbian based on both behavioral analysis—she hadn't come on to him—and symbolic reasoning. Saphie is clearly short for Sapphic, meaning lesbian, and Paradise was a clear reference to Paradise Island, home of Wonder Woman and her Amazons, lesbians all. The evidence was overwhelming, and he didn't want to repeat

his earlier faux pas. "I approve of your life choice," he muttered cautiously.

Saphie gave him a penetrating look, followed by a warm smile. "You too, big guy. Now let's see what we can find." She turned on the UV light, which glowed eerily in the semidarkness. Clear as day, written to the left of the painting, were the words "Knight Named A.H.P."

"A clue!" Hank exclaimed. "Okay, let me think." Hank scratched his head furiously, pacing up and down the room. His was the mind that had cracked Pollock's nineteenth level of meaning; no code was beyond his reach. "Got it!"

He went on. "The knight in question is Arthur Huther Pendragon, of Camelot and the round table. Clearly your grandfather wants us to go to Camelot. I'm not sure exactly where that is…"

"Actually," Saphie said gently, "it's Arthur Uther Pendragon, not Huther, and Arthur was a king, not a knight."

"Well, do you have a better idea?" Hank demanded testily.

"Mind the gap, Hank," Saphie declared.

"Say what?"

"It's an anagram. 'Knight Named A.H.P.' is an anagram for 'Mind the gap, Hank.' This message is intended for you, Hank."

"How did you do that so fast?"

"Oh, Grandfather trained me since I was a little girl. From the ages of seven to thirteen, he refused to speak with me except in anagrams."

"That's a bit sick, isn't it?" Hank ventured.

"His death!" she blurted.

"What are you talking about?"

"It's an anagram[3]," Saphie said, smiling sweetly.

---

[3] Shithead.

"We have no time for games, Saphie. What could 'mind the gap' possibly mean?" He sat on a stool, bending his fingers into a fist, putting his elbow on his knee. Lowering his chin to his fist, he assumed *The Thinker* position.

"Oh, for God's sake," Saphie muttered.

"I've got it," Hank declared. "'Mind the gap' is a colloquial phrase in an obscure English dialect known as 'British.' Translated, it means either 'pay attention to the gap' or 'don't stick your foot in a hole.' There are subtle differences (or gaps) between the San Leté painting and this Pollock. I thought they were quite understandable mistakes, but maybe these differences were deliberate. We need to study your grandfather's painting, Saphie, although I don't quite know how we're going to get to it without being noticed by McGruff."

"Will this do?" Saphie brought out a series of photographs of the crime scene, including her dead grandfather and close-ups of the faux Pollock.

"This is perfect," Hank exclaimed. "How did you get your hands on these?"

"I'm an accomplished pickpocket," she explained. "I nabbed them off the crime-fighting dog."

"Good work, Saphie. Now we need a place to hole up and do some analysis."

"I know just the place."

FOUR

I t was good to be able to relax. They had, apparently, eluded the police. They were now comfortably ensconced in the fourth-floor sitting room at the Harvard Club, a beautifully apportioned room filled with the smells of leather and cigars, and perhaps the faintest hint of vomit. Hank had laid a trace paper over the photograph of the San Leté painting. All the differences, he realized, were in the bottom left corner of the painting. From memory, he traced those elements of the painting that differed from his memory of the original.

The result was a series of thirteen star-like objects, on the left. On the right was an incomprehensible series of tiny dots. Saphie looked over his shoulder. "Stars have great symbolic value, Saphie, I get that. And thirteen is a mystical number. But these dots...that's a mystery."

"May I?" Saphie asked, taking the sheet. She took a pencil and unhesitatingly drew a series of connections between the dots. When she finished the dots on the right had taken clear form. It was a man's head, in profile, with horns and a long beard.

"Ooh, good work, Saphie. Fascinating. How did you know to connect the dots? How did you know how to? They weren't exactly numbered."

"You forget that I was raised by Eric San Leté. From the ages of ten until sixteen I was only allowed to draw in the form of connect-the-dots."

"Really?"

"Oh, yes. My grandfather clearly intended this for me."

"But what does it mean? My first guess is that it's related to Genesis, with the man being God creating the heavens. But the horns suggest a Satanic connection, or perhaps a link to the Roman demigod Pan, with implications for sexuality..." Saphie quietly turned and walked away.

"That's a bit rude," Hank muttered, but Saphie soon returned, a bottle in her hands. She handed it to him. It was an old bottle of Head & Shoulders shampoo.

"Look, everyone has a few flakes," Hank said defensively.

"Look at the logo," Saphie insisted.

Hank examined the old P&G logo on the shampoo bottle. It was unmistakably San Leté's drawing. "He's pointing us toward P&G, for some reason. There's something there we must find. You really are quite brilliant, Saphie."

Saphie gave him a little wink. "You're not so bad yourself, Hank."

"But, Saphie, what's the point of all this? Why the cloak and dagger? Why not just tell us clearly what he wants us to know?"

"All I know, Hank, is that he made an important discovery that put us both in danger. He wanted me to have his secret, but not the police."

"But what if we spend many days and risk countless dangers tracking down this secret, only to have it turn out to be a secret that your grandfather never wants revealed anyway and so all our efforts would be pointless?"

"That would be absurd, Hank," Saphie replied. "That would make no sense at all."

"Of course, you're right. I don't know what I was thinking."

"Besides, at least we're having some fun together; this is an adventure. At least, I'm having fun with you," she said shyly.

Hank gave her a penetrating look. She seemed to be coming on to him, despite his undeniable symbolic proof that she was gay. Could his analysis be wrong?

He gave her his best smile, the one he had practiced for countless hours in the mirror. "I'm having fun too, Saphie."

"So, Professor Thomas, what do you do when you aren't chasing down obscure clues?" Saphie asked.

"Oh, not much. I'm a professor of modern art at Stanford. In my spare time I've made a few billion dollars by inventing Windows, the World Wide Web, cold fusion, and spam."

Saphie eyed him coldly. "Really."

"Oh, yes, absolutely."

"I thought cold fusion didn't work."

"Oh, no, it works fine. All of Stanford is powered by a 99-cent bottle of Pepsi and a few wires," Hank replied. "It's just that it's a lot more lucrative not to make it available. You know business...so complicated." He smiled apologetically.

"And I'm pretty sure SPAM is older than you are."

"Not the meat, the nuisance e-mails. You wouldn't catch me making SPAM; that stuff is a menace."

"I see. And Microsoft doesn't own Windows?"

"They own it now, of course. Cost them a pretty penny, though, I can assure you."

"I'm impressed," Saphie conceded. "You must be quite the technical marvel."

"Not really," Hank said weakly, waving his hands in a dismissive gesture. "Just luck really..." He tried to laugh casually, but it came off as more of a choking sound.

"Well, my story is much less impressive," Saphie said. "My

early years were difficult ones. I remember nothing before my fifth birthday. Until age seven I was raised by my parents, strange and unloving people who forced us to move every seventeen days. They believed they were being hunted by aliens. They died when I was seven, and I was raised by my grandfather, a kind and loving man. When I was eleven I developed a rare disease, known as Picitis, in which the hands and feet become flipper-like and gills develop on the sides of the chest. I lived happily for years in the ocean, communicating with my grandfather only through a series of connect-the-dot pictures I drew on the beach. But after puberty I was repeatedly attacked by a gang of aggressive walruses and my life became a living hell. At age fifteen I mysteriously recovered and returned to life on the land. I am fully recovered from my trauma, except that I refuse to eat sushi and prefer not to make love in the bathtub. My grandfather arranged for me to speed learn all those missed years of school through a combination of brainwashing, electric shock and cortical injections. I now have an IQ of 215.

"In the summer before I left for my freshman year I spotted my grandfather doing something so horrific I still prefer not to think about it. Although on reflection there may have been multiple interpretations for what I saw. I have not communicated with him since. I excelled at Harvard, where my intellect allowed me to easily dominate my peers. I am now a senior, majoring in Strident Feminism and the Divine Feminine, and am currently working on my final thesis, tentatively titled 'All Sexual Intercourse is Rape'."

Hank gulped. "Tough room," he muttered.

Saphie gave him a sweet and innocent smile. "To Cincinnati, then?"

Meanwhile, the Poodle sat at police headquarters with his two key lieutenants, Joe "The Bunny" Mason and Frankie "Chihuahua" Rosenstein. Everything was going according to plan. "Okay, gentlemen," he stated grandly, "our fish are hooked. Let's see where they are headed, shall we? Sergeant Mason, will you do the honors?"

Mason fired up the computer, which showed a map of the city. There, in glowing white phosphorus, was nothing at all. "Well," the Poodle yelled, "where are they?"

"Not sure, boss. The bug Frankie planted doesn't seem to be working."

"Wait a minute," Rosenstein said defensively, "you were supposed to plant the bug."

"No, today is the thirteenth, an odd-numbered day, so that makes it your turn."

"Yes, but it's also a prime, which..."

The Poodle, his face an alarming shade of red, stormed out, heading for the emergency room. He was determined to get there ahead of the heart attack, for once. *Damn*, he thought, *this happens every single time...*

They arrived in Cincinnati at midday and decided to spend time at a local diner, Sally's Place, until evening when they would break into P&G headquarters. Saphie killed time by reciting various anagrams for Sally's Place:

Scalps Alley
Classy lapel!
Play ass? Cell!
A sly scalpel
As calls yelp
Spell as clay
Pascal yells!
A spa cell? Sly!
Yell salsa! PC?
All ply cases
Cal slaps Ely
Scylla pleas
Laps call, yes?
Call apes? Sly!
Clap ass. Yell!
All yes? Scalp!

"Yes, yes, you are quite good at that," Hank said tiredly. "But can we do something else?"

"Sure," Saphie said agreeably. "You want to tell me how you really made billions of dollars?"

He looked at her. She really was very lovely. *But can I trust her?* Somehow he felt that he could. "I'll tell you, but it has to be our secret."

"Cross my heart," she promised.

"To understand how I made my money you have to understand the nature of modern art. I'll start with the most basic principle of modern art: it sucks."

"Hold on, modern art doesn't 'suck.' It just requires a more sophisticated sense of aesthetic appreciation than earlier forms of art."

"That's actually a common misconception. Modern art does 'suck,' if by 'suck' we mean that it fails to have any relationship to natural human aesthetics, sense of beauty or transcendence. Humans naturally respond to art; that's why we've been making art for at least 40,000 years. But it's only in the last hundred years or so that the purpose of art has completely changed. Art is no longer about beauty or aesthetics; it's about codes. Modern artists bury layer upon layer of meaning in their paintings. The more sophisticated and deeper the layers of meaning, the more respected the artist is by the inner circle of artists and critics in the know. But beauty has nothing to do with it. A Mondrian painting has more in common with a crossword puzzle than it does with the Mona Lisa."

"But I have friends, art majors, who find great beauty in modern art."

"No you don't. They're either lying to you or to themselves. No one can find beauty in modern art because *it isn't there*. It isn't supposed to be there. But no one is going to buy a $200,000

Jackson Pollock if he thinks it's essentially a glorified Jumble Puzzle, is he? So the inner circle pretends to see beauty for the sake of the plebes, and holds out the hope that one can learn enough to see the beauty. Many pretend to, because seeing the beauty is considered a sign of sophistication. But to those in the know, it's a big joke."

"A mean one if you ask me. Well, what does this have to do with making billions of dollars?"

"You know that Jackson Pollock is one of the most celebrated artists of the century, yes? Pollock was legendary for inscribing eighteen separate layers of meaning in each of his paintings, each completely different and each referring to the lower levels. Naturally they look like crap, even by the standards of modern art. How could they not? Pollock was a prankster, too. Do you know that he actually pretended that he created his masterpieces by letting paint drip out of a can *randomly*? Complete nonsense. Pollock controlled every atom of paint that touched his canvas; he was more precise than Da Vinci."

Saphie cleared her throat politely.

"Yes, to the point. One day, about twenty years ago, I discovered Pollock's nineteenth layer of meaning. I was studying *Shimmering Substance*, one of his lesser works, when I suddenly made a series of connections that no one had made before. Before I knew it, I had the recipe for Superglue."

"But that would have been in the '80s. But I thought Superglue's been around a lot longer than that."

"You are quite correct, Saphie. I couldn't make any money off Superglue because it had already been invented. But *Shimmering Substance* was painted in 1946, long before Harry Coover invented Superglue. I raced to other paintings. In *Number 8, 1949* I found all the technical requirements to build the World Wide Web."

"Hold on, Tim Berners-Lee invented the Web."

"Funny story, that. Timmy and I were drunk off our asses in Morocco. In a fit of comradeship, I gave him the whole thing."

"You gave him the World Wide Web?"

"Well, it was just an idea then. I never made a dime off it, but then again, neither did Tim, really. Anyway, after that I was off. In *Lavender Mist* I found the source code for Windows; not Pollock's best work if you ask me, although Bill did quite well with it. In *Mural* I found the design blueprints for cold fusion. In *Autumn Rhythm* I discovered a method for causing the sun to go nova; I've kept that one to myself so far. And so on. That's my secret; I'm not an inventor at all. I'm really a fraud, if you think about it."

"It's true that you didn't invent these things, but you did discover the nineteenth layer. That took some doing." Saphie gave him an encouraging smile.

"That's true enough," Hank admitted. "Anyway, that's the whole story. Now you know everything."

"Not quite everything, Hank. You haven't answered the most interesting question of all. How the hell did Jackson Pollock know all that stuff?"

"You know, I never thought of that..."

The Procter & Gamble building was a glass fortress. Surprisingly, for a corporate headquarters, there were eight armed guards clearly visible in the large, ornate reception area. Undoubtedly many more lurked out of sight. It was clear to Hank that trying to get in through the lobby would be pointless.

"I'll get to the roof and drop a line down the back of the building. You climb up and we're in easy as pie," Saphie suggested.

"You'll get to the roof? Get to the roof? The sides of the building are sheer glass. How will you possibly get to the roof?" Hank almost stuttered these questions.

Saphie pointed at the stream that ran by the back of the building. "I'll jump into there, swim up into the plumbing system, get out in a utility room, disable the alarms, get to the roof and that's that," Saphie explained.

Hank stared at her uncomprehendingly.

She smiled apologetically. "Residual gills, you know."

Soon they were both at the entrance to Procter & Gamble's cavernous secret vault, located in the southwest corner of the building's basement (Hank had cleverly realized the implications of the fact that San Leté had put the P&G symbol in the lower left corner of his painting).

The vault door was eight feet high and four feet wide, with an enormous dial in the center. It was clearly impenetrable. Hank knelt by the knob, put a glass against the door, and began spinning the dial.

"What are you doing?" Saphie demanded.

"Shhh. I saw this in a movie once," Hank replied.

Saphie waited a minute, then said, "Hank."

"Quiet, Saphie."

"Hank, what do you say we try the numbers Grandfather gave us?"

"Do you think they might have an obscure correspondence to letters in the Aramaic alphabet?"

"Actually, I think they might be the combination."

Saphie reached over and spun the dial five times. The door slowly swung open.

"That was easy," Hank said sourly.

The interior of the vault looked like nothing so much as the government warehouse in the final scene of *Raiders of the Lost Ark*. There were row after row of sealed boxes, each labeled only with a brief description. Saphie shined her flashlight around in confusion.

"Now what?" Saphie asked. "We don't know what we're looking for, never mind where it is."

"I have an idea. Look for anything labeled 'Rubik's Cube' or 'Alien Weapon.'"

"Good thinking, Hank."

Between them they found cures for baldness, dandruff and blondness, a colorless cream that gave a baby-smooth shave that lasts for years, and a box labeled *Anal Probe Lubricant*. Finally, they found what they were looking for: a one-foot square box labeled *Rubik's Cube*. Hank took it down, unknowingly triggering a silent alarm.

Inside was an ordinary Rubik's Cube.

"Obviously we are meant to solve this cube," Hank said, twisting frantically.

After a few minutes of this, Saphie asked, "You want me to do this? By now I could have solved it with my feet."

"I doubt that," Hank muttered.

Saphie took the cube and gracefully sat down on the concrete floor of the vault. She slipped off her stylish Tod's loafers. Her feet were quite pretty and her long toes easily picked up the cube and began twisting.

"Is this really necessary?" Hank groaned.

"Done!" Saphie said cheerfully. She placed the cube on the ground between her legs. As soon as her feet released the cube it began falling apart, decomposing into a pile of smaller cubes. In the center there was a delicate scroll of paper. Saphie reached in with her toes and carefully took the paper. With both feet she carefully unrolled the paper, more gracefully, Hank was forced to admit, than he could have done with his hands.

"I think you made your point," Hank said sourly.

"It's a letter to me," Saphie declared. She read:

```
Eric San Leté
Grand Pubah
The Ancient Order of the Masons


Dearest Saphie,
    If you are reading this, then my enemies have tak-
en me out of the picture and I have left a clue that
only you could follow. That clue led you here. I am
sorry to burden you with this, but you are the key
to solving a problem that has plagued our race since
time immemorial.
    There has been a conspiracy going for a very long
time, a conspiracy so vast and so profound that it
makes the conspiracy in The Da Vinci Code (for ex-
ample) seem like child's play.
    It's absolutely critical that you understand the
truth, and that you take action to prevent a global
calamity. Everything depends on it.
    I have developed a weapon of devastating power;
```

you are the key to it. With this weapon my enemies
will be stopped…if you help me now.
    I could explain it all in this letter, but for
complex psychological reasons I think it's best that
I just give you another obscure clue, this time in
the form of a haiku:

    Find four with three sides
    And one with four...the tallest
    Go all the way down

    Your loving father,
    Eric

"That's very bizarre," Hank observed. "I thought Eric was your grandfather."

"He is. I don't know why he says he's my father, except maybe to remind me that he's been like a father to me."

"Your grandfather was Grand Pubah of the Masons? What problem plagued our race? What conspiracy is he talking about? What weapon could he have possibly developed? What does the Haiku refer to?"

"I don't know the answer to any of these questions. All I know is that, as a child, I explored my grandfather's closet, a place he had told me to stay out of. I discovered a very grand hat. When I asked my grandfather about it, he scolded me for going into the closet, but told me that was his Grand Pubah hat, and that it had great symbolic significance."

"This could be very important, Saphie. What did this hat look like?"

"It was very tall, maybe twelve inches high, and cylindrical in shape. On the front was a circle sitting on a crescent shape, with the crescent facing upward. It was covered with fur and had horns coming out of the sides," Saphie described.

"Isn't that from *The Flintstones*?" Hank asked dubiously.

"Hanging from one of the horns was a key. On it were the initials 'PS.' When I asked Grandfather about it he just laughed it off, calling it his 'pastrami key,' whatever that means. But I could tell he wished I hadn't seen it."

"Saphie, this is huge. Your grandfather must have been the leader of the Pastrami Sandwich Society, known as PS. We must find that key."

"I have it, Hank. McGruff gave it to me; it was one of Grandfather's personal effects."

Suddenly the lights came on. A loud voice declared, "Stay where you are, there is no way to escape. Cooperate and no one gets hurt."

Saphie stood quickly and grabbed Hank's arm. She pointed at what seemed to be a large drain fifty feet ahead. She ran toward it, dragging him behind her. The drain was solidly mounted in the concrete. "You'll never lift that," Hank observed.

"*Turn around with your hands raised*," a voice behind him ordered.

Hank turned slowly, arms raised, and saw a security guard approaching him, weapon drawn, from fifty feet away. "Get behind me," he said.

From behind him he heard a tremendous wrench of steel and ripping of concrete, and he knew that Saphie had somehow opened the drain. "I'm not really much of a swimmer," Hank muttered nervously.

He felt a sharp tug on his pants and he fell backward into the cold water. He heard a shot ring out, and found himself sinking into the water. Then everything went black.

NINE

The guard looked down at the water that had swallowed up the two trespassers. The boss would be furious, but there was no chance of catching them now. He went back to his desk and dialed a number that only a handful of people had access to. The phone was picked up immediately. He cleared his throat. "Karl, I'm afraid I have some bad news."

Hank dreamed he was lying on a luxurious bed, and the most beautiful girl in the world was kissing him frantically, then rubbing his chest, then kissing him, then rubbing his chest with somewhat painful force, then kissing him, then pushing his chest hard enough to crack a rib...

He woke, choking and spitting water. Saphie sat beside him on the grass, looking concerned.

"You okay?"

"Never better," Hank declared, and realized that it was true. "By the way, I've used my time unconscious quite effectively. I've solved the haiku."

"Do tell."

"We're to go to the lowest level of the Great Pyramid of Cheops, in Egypt."

"Really?"

"Oh, yes, it's quite obvious really," Hank said, unsuccessfully trying not to sound pompous. "The hard part will be getting access to the Great Pyramid. The Egyptian government is a little particular about who gains entrance."

"I have an idea about that," Saphie said.

At the Cincinnati Airport, Saphie and Hank were standing in a long line waiting to get through security. In front of them, four young Arabic-looking men were chanting "Death to the Great Satan." They passed through security without incident.

"That's a bit unnerving," Hank confessed. "But still, I'm glad to see that we aren't discriminating on our security procedures. Although I do wonder if that's really necessary." He pointed to their left, where an elderly woman was being patted down as her wheelchair was disassembled.

Just then a beefy security guard walked up. "Sir, are you criticizing our security procedures?"

"Oh, no, not at all, officer." Hank said weakly, "I was just joking."

"You were *what*?"

"Uh, joking?"

The guard spoke into his radio. "I'm going to need some help here."

"You don't need help," Hank protested.

Hank was surrounded by three security guards, who dragged him to the front of the line. The first guard pointed to a sign. "What does that say?"

"Airport security is not a joking matter," Hank admitted.

Hank soon found himself surrounded by security guards in a windowless gray room, bare except for a large table in the center. The senior guard was an evil-looking woman with a prominent mole on the left side of her nose. Her name-tag read "Helga."

Hank's Tumi roll-on bag was put on a metal table. Helga opened the bag and pulled out a large white elastic cloth. "What's this?"

"That's my belly buster," Hank muttered.

"You wear a girdle?" Helga laughed maliciously.

"It's a belly buster," Hank insisted.

Helga began pulling out bottles. "Facial Regenerator," she read. "Hydrating Face Wash, Energy Face Scrub, Vital Body Moisturizer, Power Face Mask, No Friction Shave Crème, Balance Aftershave Gel, Shaving Nick Cover Stick..."

Helga chose a bottle at random, opened it, smelled it, and wrinkled her nose. "What is this stuff?"

"I have delicate skin," Hank protested. "Those are all legitimate products."

Helga reached in again. "Miracle Hair Gro, Viagra, Penile Growth pills." She stopped. "Now what do we have here? Ground rhino horn. This stuff is illegal, bud."

"That's made exclusively from rhinos who have died from natural causes."

"Tell it to the judge."

She reached in again and pulled out a set of schematics. She looked through the papers, her eyes widening in astonishment. "These are blueprints for a neutron bomb." She grinned wickedly. "We caught ourselves a terrorist."

"I'm not a terrorist. Those are just from an art project I'm working on. I know it looks kind of bad..."

"Let's see what else you got in here, terrorist." She dumped the bag over on the table and rummaged through it.

"Nothing else, really," Hank pleaded.

"We'll see. Now comes the fun part." She pulled on a rubber glove with a distinctive snap. "Strip."

Hank gulped.

—————————————————————

TWELVE

Hank and Saphie settled into their first-class seats on the flight to Cairo. Hank still looked somewhat shaky. "I thought they were going to arrest me for sure. They kept calling me a terrorist."

"Well, maybe you shouldn't travel with plans for a neutron bomb on you. I can't believe they let you go."

"Apparently something more important came up. They got a phone call and just let me go."

"So, Hank," Saphie asked, "what do you think Grandfather meant by 'Oh, Alien Weapon'? Was it a joke or some kind of puzzle? You don't think he meant, alien, like aliens?" She formed her forefingers into antennae in explanation. "I mean, there are no aliens; that's nonsense, right?"

"Actually, Saphie, that's a common misconception."

Saphie frowned slightly at this, but Hank didn't notice. He was in full lecture mode now. "There almost certainly are aliens. Cosmologists have calculated that there must be thousands, more likely millions, of alien civilizations in the universe. Consider that there are roughly 100 billion galaxies in the universe that we know of, and roughly 100 billion stars in the galaxy, that means that there are 10,000 billion billion stars in the universe, an inconceivable number. Odds are quite a few of those stars developed life."

"That doesn't necessarily follow," Saphie protested. "Most of those stars probably don't even have planets."

"That's true, but astronomers are finding that lots of stars have planets. If only one in 100 stars have planets, that's still 100 billion billion stars with planets."

"But what are the odds that life will develop on these planets?"

"Quite good, actually, at least on planets similar to Earth. Life developed on Earth almost immediately after Earth's formation, suggesting that the development of life is quite a common occurrence, at least on Earth-like planets. So if even only one in a billion planets is like Earth, that still leaves us with 100 billion stars with life. If only one in a million planets with life develops intelligent life, that's still 100 million planets with intelligent alien life."

"Okay, smarty pants, so if the universe is lousy with aliens, where are they?"

"Well, Saphie, you've just expressed a neat summary of Fermi's Paradox," Hank intoned. "Enrico Fermi, one of the last century's greatest physicists, asked just this question. As it turns out, there are only three possible answers."

"One, they've chosen not to communicate with us. This is possible, but very unlikely. What are the odds that 100 million different alien races would all agree not to communicate with us?"

"Two, they are out communicating with us but we are misinterpreting or not understanding their messages. Again, this seems unlikely. We've been broadcasting radio into space for decades. If they wanted to crack our language, they could have done it by now."

"So what's the third option?"

"The third option is that the aliens are here, but for some reason they don't want us to know about it."

THIRTEEN

New York City's Little Italy is filled with cobblestone roads and humble tenement buildings. A casual visitor walking through this unpretentious neighborhood would be startled to find an incongruously placed Baroque-revival-style palace at 240 Centre Street. This ornate structure was designed in 1909 by Hoppin & Koen. At that time, architects and planners still paid homage to the image of the "White City," the Beaux Arts idea of the perfect city that had been displayed at the World's Columbian Exposition in Chicago in 1893.

The building's dome harkens to the great cupola of the Hotel des Invalides in Paris, albeit not quite so ornate. But its wedge-shape at the north end also evokes memories of Venice and its great promontory buildings.[4]

240 Centre Street is the headquarters of New York's vaunted police department. In his large office on the top story, the Poodle gave a satisfied laugh. *What chance did a Harvard co-ed and a French art historian have against the legendary NYPD?* He

---

[4] Oh yes, a great deal of research went into this book, with many laboriously described true details added for extra credibility. It makes the whole book that much more plausible, don't you think?

couldn't wait until he had them both in custody. He would give them one of his legendary Sipowicz-style interrogations. Fortunately, their mistakes at airport security allowed him to instruct the security officials to hide a new tracker beacon in their luggage. Egyptian police, working with his men in New York, would track them to their Cairo location and unearth the entire conspiracy behind San Leté's death. This would be the biggest coup of his career.

Suddenly, he received a call. He listened carefully for a few minutes, then called his men, Joe and Frankie, into his office. "Joe, inform the Egyptian authorities that we were mistaken about Thomas. We're going to head out to Cairo ourselves."

"Cairo, boss?" Frankie asked. "Isn't that a little outside our jurisdiction?"

McGruff glared at his subordinates. "Get with the program, gentlemen. We're Americans. No place on Earth is outside our authority."

FOURTEEN

"There's another possibility, Hank," Saphie suggested. "God created man as the only intelligent race in the universe."

"Oh, please," Hank protested. "You don't believe in all that God nonsense, do you? This is the 21st century. No rational person uses 'God' to explain the features of the natural universe."

"If God doesn't exist, why does ninety-five percent of humanity believe in Him? Surely that shows that there is some truth to these beliefs, *n'est pas*?[5]"

"Actually, Saphie, that's a common misconception," Hank explained condescendingly. Saphie gritted her teeth but said nothing. "The number of people who believe in something proves nothing. One hundred percent of the human race once believed the Earth was flat. That didn't make it flat. Obviously at some point in our evolutionary history it turned out to be advantageous to believe in some sort of mystical nonsense and so now..."

Just then the plane lurched suddenly and began to shake. An

---

[5] She's French, remember?

44

announcement went through the cabin. "*We are experiencing some turbulence. Please fasten your seatbelts.*"

Hank looked out the window and saw smoke coming from one of the two engines on the right side of the plane. "Oh my God, Saphie, do you see that?" Hank asked.

Saphie raised an eyebrow. "So you are calling on God now? I suggest a quiet prayer." Saphie closed her eyes.

"It's an expression, Saphie," Hank said. "Do you really think God is holding the plane up? Don't be ridiculous. If there's a God, what's He hiding for? Why doesn't He give us an unambiguous sign of His existence? If there's a God, I demand an unambiguous sign!"

Immediately the smoking engine burst into flames. The plane lurched again, and the angle of their decent steepened. Hank stared at it in amazement and Saphie glared at him. "Are you satisfied now?" Saphie asked.

"That proves nothing. That engine was already smoking. I demand a truly unambiguous sign!"

The second engine on the right wing burst into flames. Saphie whirled on Hank furiously. "Can you please stop challenging God until we are on the ground?"

"Okay," Hank murmured nervously.

FIFTEEN

The sprawling 534-acre estate of Pemberley was located 35 miles south of Cairo. The owner, a lovably eccentric and extravagantly rich Englishman, Sir Richard Villain, had torn down an ancient Egyptian temple to make room for a brick-by-brick recreation of England's classic Pemberley Mansion. Since Pemberley didn't actually exist, Villain had the local builders recreate the mansion based on its portrayal in BBC's revered *Pride & Prejudice* miniseries.

Among the most important of Villain's projects was the recreation, on the back acres of his property, of the Giza Pyramids, using only "slave" labor and the original methods. The Giza Pyramids were a miracle of construction and precision, and many Egyptologists maintained that they couldn't possibly have been built with the technologies available to Egyptians at that time (that, in fact, they would be daunting to construct with today's technologies). Villain's project was an attempt to prove them wrong.

Saphie drove quietly down the dusty Cairo roads in their rented MG convertible, Hank seated beside her. The top was down and the drive to Pemberley was pleasant, if a bit dusty. Saphie drove contently as she remembered many a happy day

in her youth with her grandfather and Uncle Rich, scribbling anagrams on the beach. Uncle Rich's dogsbody, Traitor McSneaky, would always bring a bucket of fish for her. Oh, the fun they had!

Uncle Rich was always kind and helpful, and Saphie was sure he would do everything he could to get them access to the secret basement of the Great Pyramid. With his contacts in the Egyptian ministries, it should be quite easy for him. But he was a bit of an eccentric, and she shuddered to think what hurdles he would make her jump before they were given access to the mansion.

Saphie drove up to the driveway entrance. One of Villain's eccentricities was that the speaker system was on the passenger side and five feet off the ground. Saphie crawled over Hank, her knees awkwardly squeezed between his thighs, her shapely buttocks inches from his face. Hank became uncomfortably aware of Saphie's presence, but resolved to be the perfect gentleman.

Saphie pressed the speaker button. "Uncle Rich?" she asked. "It's Saphie. I need your help."

"This is Traitor McSneaky, Sir Villain's most abused dogsbody. Welcome back to Pemberley, Saphie. I'll have one of the servants run to the market and get some fresh fish for you."

"Thank you, Traitor, but that won't be necessary. I'm off sushi. But it's critical that I speak with Uncle Rich immediately."

"That won't be possible, Saphie. He's busy disciplining one of his 'slaves.' You know how he hates to be interrupted in his discipline sessions."

"Traitor, tell him that I have critical information that Grandfather left me just before his death. This won't wait."

"And tell him…" Hank began. Saphie leaned backward, pressing her right buttock into Hank's face, effectively cutting off further words.

"It's best if I handle this," Saphie said apologetically. "Uncle Rich can be a little tricky."

Hank was overwhelmed by Saphie's presence. He couldn't help being attracted to her despite her lesbian predilections, and he soon found, to his horror, that his manhood, awkwardly pressed against her knees, was beginning to assert itself.

Saphie looked down at Hank quizzically. "Really, Hank," she said with a slight smile on her face. "I appreciate the thought, but this really isn't a good time." With that she pulled her knee back and rammed it heavily into Hank's crotch, solving his erection problem and leaving him gasping for air.

"Saphie!" It was Sir Villain on the speakerphone. "I'm delighted you've come. Is anyone with you?"

"Yes, Uncle Rich. Hank Thomas, one of the foremost art historians in the United States, is with me."

"Pleased to meet you, Dr. Thomas," Villain said graciously.

"He can't talk right now, Uncle Rich." Indeed, Hank was doubled over his seat, wheezing heavily. "Let us in and I'll explain everything."

"You know the routine, Saphie. First you must answer three questions for me."

"Yes, Uncle Rich," Saphie said resignedly.

"First question," asked Villain with obvious pleasure. "What shall I serve at dinner, stink heads or a Maasai special?"

Saphie thought furiously. Stink heads, she knew, were a traditional Eskimo delicacy of fish heads buried a few months to ferment. A Maasai special was the traditional Maasai meal of cow blood and fermented milk. A dedicated anthropologist, Uncle Rich had lived among both the Eskimo and the Maasai at various points in his distinguished career and was quite obsessed with their odd delicacies.

Saphie suddenly remembered that Uncle Rich now swore by

the Atkins diet, and thus refused milk in any form. "The stink heads, Uncle Rich," she declared triumphantly. "Although Hank and I are both vegetarians," she added.

Hank made as if to disagree, but Saphie shook her head insistently. "Trust me on this," she whispered.

"Excellent, Saphie," Villain conceded. "Second question. What is the last time America beat England on the field of battle?"

"Well, there's . . ." Hank began, but quickly subsided when Saphie lifted her knee threateningly.

"That would be never, Uncle Rich," Saphie replied.

"Quite correct, my girl. Excellent," Villain intoned with pleasure. "Final question, and this is a matter of grave importance. What," he asked gleefully, "is the airborne velocity of an unladen swallow?"

Saphie knew this one. "Would that be an African or a European swallow, Uncle Rich?"

"Good answer! You are still San Leté's true granddaughter. Please enter."

The magnificent iron gates slowly opened. They drove in.

The door to Pemberley opened just as Saphie and Hank approached. Standing there was a miserable-looking man in his mid-thirties, dressed in what seemed to be dirty rags. His eyes protruded noticeably in his round face, and he bore a vague resemblance to Peter Lorre.

"Welcome, Mistress Paradise. Welcome, pompous bald American whose name I do not know."

Saphie giggled. "Oh, stop that, Traitor. You're always so grouchy. This is Hank Thomas, one of America's foremost art historians. Hank, this is Traitor McSneaky, my uncle's dogsbody."

McSneaky gave an awkward combination of bow and prostration. "It's a pleasure to meet you, Master Thomas," he muttered. He didn't seem particularly pleased.

"What's a dogsbody?" Hank asked.

"I do whatever chores are too unpleasant for the slaves," McSneaky said miserably.

Hank looked at Saphie. She shrugged.

"So how have you been, Traitor?" Saphie asked. "Life treating you well?"

"Oh, it's all bunnies and roses here at Pemberley. Why, only yesterday I had the privilege of licking clean all of the chamber pots."

"Is that sanitary?" Hank whispered to Saphie.

"He's just kidding, Hank," Saphie replied, although she didn't look quite certain.

They followed the dogsbody through the massive hallway.

SIXTEEN

The Poodle was not happy. The Egyptian slave robes he had rented in order to sneak into Pemberley were too small, and were unable to fully cover his substantial belly. The heat was miserable, and Frankie and Joe would not stop their inane chatter.

"So is fifteen a prime?" Joe was asking.

"Quiet, you two," McGruff demanded. They had successfully made it onto the grounds, but now they had the much more challenging job of sneaking into the house. They had to overhear what was being said; Rove had given him strict instructions that Hank and Saphie were not to be arrested until they revealed the location of the weapon.

They had almost made it to the back doors when they were stopped by Villain's overseer. "Where the hell do you slaves think you're going?"

"The Master has asked us to do some work for him in the house," McGruff improvised.

"Nonsense," the overseer exclaimed. "The Master never lets slaves in the house." He cracked his whip threateningly. "Come on, you dirty slaves, this camel shit won't shovel itself."

SEVENTEEN

Traitor led them into a grand main room. They sat on an antique sofa that could easily accommodate five, and waited anxiously for Villain to arrive.

He soon appeared at the top of the ornate spiral staircase. He was dressed in the robes of an Egyptian Pharaoh and slowly descended the staircase. Four barely dressed servant girls descended backward in front of him, waving enormous fans, and scattering rose petals at his feet.

"That Uncle Rich, he loves to make an entrance," Saphie giggled.

Villain reached the bottom of the stairs and entered the room. "My dearest Saphie," he exclaimed, enthusiastically embracing her in his arms. "I'm so sorry about Eric."

Villain turned to Thomas. "And you must be the renowned art scholar Hank Thomas," Villain continued.

"That's me," Hank said modestly.

"Sit, sit. Saphie, Dr. Thomas. I'm delighted you are here, but you've intrigued me. Something about critical information from Eric?"

"Well, it's a bit of a complicated story, Uncle Rich."

"Go back to the beginning, Saphie. I'm in no rush."

"As you know, I have no memory of anything before my fifth birthday. On that day..."

"Not that far back, Saphie."

"Okay. Three days ago I received a series of messages from Grandfather telling me we were both in grave danger. Naturally I ignored this, despite the fact that San Leté was legendary for his honesty. But then he was found dead and a secret code led us to this letter." Saphie handed him the letter. Villain read it silently.

"Now Hank thinks we need to go to the basement of the Great Pyramid to find Grandfather's secret. We need your help getting access," Saphie concluded.

"I can help, Saphie," Villain agreed. "But how much do you really know about the pyramids? Dr. Thomas, you are privy to these secrets, I'm sure. Have you revealed to Saphie the secrets of the pyramids?"

"We didn't really have time," Hank confessed. "I only got as far as Fermi's Paradox."

"Well, well, well," Villain said delightedly. "We have a virgin."

"A virgin is a reference to anyone who isn't privy to the secrets of the pyramids," Hank explained apologetically.

"We're going to pop your cherry tonight!" Villain exclaimed with glee. "We're going to plow your field, deflower your ignorance. We're going to depredate, desecrate and deflorate. The Martian probe of knowledge is going to penetrate the tight clouds of Venus."

Hank felt slightly uncomfortable with Villain's risqué analogies, and attempted to change the topic. "About the pyramids, Sir Villain..."

"We're going to brutally pierce your hymen of ignorance, Saphie," Villain continued, ignoring Hank. "We're going to rip through..."

"Okay, Uncle Rich, I get it," Saphie said with irritation. "You know something I don't. Grow up."

Villain didn't look the least bit abashed. "Saphie, what you first need to understand is that the pyramids of Egypt couldn't possibly have been built with the resources and technologies available to the Egyptians," Villain explained.

"I know it wasn't easy. But surely with a huge army of slaves it was possible," Saphie complained.

"That's actually a common misconception..." Hank began, but cut off as Saphie glared at him.

"Dr. Thomas is right, Saphie. You need to appreciate just how huge the pyramids are. They were the highest buildings ever constructed until the building of the Eiffel Tower. The Great Pyramid is almost a tenth of a mile high, and covers an area of almost half a million square feet. The perimeter is over half a mile around. It's built from 2.5 million limestone blocks, each with an average weight of 2.5 tons. The Great Pyramid alone weighs over six million tons; that means that, with no powered equipment whatsoever, the Egyptians somehow built a six-million-ton building going almost a tenth of a mile high. The Great Pyramid is over seventeen times as heavy as the Empire State Building, which was considered a miracle of engineering when built with the technology of the 1930s. Some of the granite blocks and pillars in the Valley Temple are over 200 tons each. When you consider that not until the 1970s did we have cranes that could lift even 100 tons, the sheer impossibility of what the Egyptians supposedly built becomes clearer."

"And when you consider," Hank added, "that the nearest source of granite was Aswan, 600 miles to the south. How did they get ton after ton of granite hundreds of miles... just to build one of many temples?"

"It's amazing, I admit," Saphie conceded, "but with enough

time and enough slaves... I thought you were building a pyra-mid here at Pemberley just to show it can be done."

"Oh, that. No, I'm not serious about recreating the Great Pyr-amid. It couldn't be done, not for all of my wealth. That's really just an excuse to have my own slaves," Villain admitted. "But there was a serious effort to do just that. Recently, Egyptolo-gist Mark Lehner attempted to build a model of a true pyramid. They soon gave up trying to quarry and move the stone blocks using the soft copper tools that were all the Egyptians had avail-able. So Lehner used modern tools to cut and move the stones. Lehner's team ultimately cut 186 blocks, each weighing con-siderably less than the stones in the Great Pyramid, and barely managed to build a pyramid that was only slightly taller than a man. If anything, all our modern efforts to recreate the work of the Egyptians have only validated just how impossible it was.

"But it's not just a matter of brute force. The Egyptians knew things they couldn't have known," Villain continued. "The Great Pyramid is aligned to the points of the compass with un-canny precision. The ratio of the perimeter to the height of the pyramid is a multiple of pi, to six decimal places! And the ratio of the slant height to the base is phi, otherwise known as the golden mean."

"That is impressive," Saphie conceded.

"It's more than impressive," Villain declared. "*It's impossible.* Euclid discovered phi thousands of years after the Great Pyra-mid was built. The Egyptians couldn't possibly have had the knowledge needed to build the Great Pyramid."

"How can that be?" Saphie asked.

"There's more. The three pyramids of Giza form a pattern on the ground that aligns almost exactly with the three belt stars of the Orion Belt."

"Almost perfectly... it could be a coincidence."

"True," Villain replied, "except for the fact that the pyramids lined up exactly in the year 10,450 B.C. This is long before the pyramids were originally thought to have been built, but there's increasing evidence that the pyramids are far older than we suspected, which makes their construction all that more miraculous. And there's the matter of why the Great Pyramid was built at all."

"It's a tomb, isn't it?" Saphie asked.

"That's actually a common misconception," Hank muttered under his breath. Louder, he added, "There's never been any trace of a tomb found in the Great Pyramid."

"Fine, so if the Egyptians couldn't have built the pyramids, who did? Aliens?"

"Pop!" Villain exclaimed with glee. "Exactly, Saphie. I believe Hank already explained about Fermi's Paradox. From what we know about the universe, the most likely scenario is that aliens are here, but hidden. But the legacy of the Egyptians reveals that they were hidden, but still quite active."

"Maybe the Egyptians were more advanced than we thought. How do we know it was aliens?"

"It's more than just the miraculous building of the pyramids," Hank interjected. "There is considerable evidence that pyramids and other structures were built to be viewed from a great height. And there's the matter of the pyramids found on Mars."

"Mars?" Saphie asked doubtfully.

"That's right, Saphie," Villain said. "Images of Mars' surface taken by the Mariner 9 probe, and later confirmed by the Viking probe, show a series of pyramids on the Martian surface. No theory of Martian geology can explain these. Further, faces in Egyptian headdress can clearly be seen on the Martian surface."

"You have to be kidding."

"Not at all. Traitor, bring me my Mars file." Traitor, who had been standing quietly in the corner, shuffled to the enormous bank of file cabinets in one corner of the room and pulled out one file. He brought it over to Villain with a grunt. Villain pulled two photos from the file and handed them to Saphie. They were labeled "Viking Probe photographs."

Saphie examined the photographs, particularly a structure labeled "The D&M Pyramid." It sure looked like a pyramid. The other photo showed an area of the Martian surface that looked suspiciously like an Egyptian headdress. "This is amazing, Uncle Rich," she exclaimed. "How is this not known?"

"Every Egyptologist worth his salt knows that the pyramids were built by aliens, Saphie. But it's not exactly a fast-track to tenure to go around saying so."

"So what happened to these aliens?"

"Well, as far as we can tell, Egyptian civilization was essentially an alien artifact, and the aliens were gods to humans, and treated as such. But with the fall of the Egyptian dynasties and the rise of independent civilizations like the Greeks, the aliens went underground, though they never lost sight of their goal of dominating the human race. There are some that believe that the early Christian church was actually dominated by aliens in another attempt to rule humanity through religion," Villain explained.

"So Jesus was an alien?" Saphie asked doubtfully.

"Certainly Da Vinci thought so," Hank interjected.

"Da Vinci? What does he have to do with any of this?" Saphie asked.

"Da Vinci was a brilliant thinker," Villain said. "He certainly believed that the early Church was dominated by aliens. For his own safety he hid his knowledge, but he provided numerous clues in his paintings."

Villain stood up and went to a corner of the room where a large purple curtain hung. He pulled the ropes of the curtain, which opened to reveal a large painting. "Do you recognize this?" he asked.

Saphie and Hank walked toward the painting. "That's a reproduction of Da Vinci's *Last Supper*, isn't it?"

Villain snorted. "Reproduction, hell. The one in Milan's the reproduction. This is the original."

"That's impressive," Hank admitted. "You won't believe the trouble I went through obtaining the *Mona Lisa*."

"Saphie, take a close look at Jesus," Villain requested.

"What, is he really a woman?" Saphie asked jokingly.

"Not quite," Villain responded. He handed her a large magnifying glass. "Try this."

Saphie examined the painting through the glass. At first she saw nothing unusual; then suddenly she spotted it. Two antennae were rising from Jesus' head. They were the same color as the blue background and were easy to miss, but once spotted they were unmistakable.

"But, Uncle Rich, how could Da Vinci have known about this?"

Villain smiled like a cat that had just swallowed a canary. "He knew," Villain explained, "because he was one of them."

E I G H T E E N

"What?" Saphie and Hank exclaimed simultaneously.

Villain was enjoying their confusion. "That's right, there's considerable evidence that Da Vinci was one of the aliens. In his notebooks he refers to the creators of mankind living among us; this was thought to be some obscure heresy, but now we think these 'creators' are the aliens. Then we discovered the hidden Michelangelo paintings."

"You're losing me, Uncle Rich."

"It's simple. In his notebooks Da Vinci refers to the creators, saying 'you shall know them by their moles.' Obviously the aliens were otherwise indistinguishable from humans."

"What does this have to do with Michelangelo?"

"Seven years ago a hidden stash of Michelangelo paintings was discovered. Naturally I bought them. As you may know, both Da Vinci and Michelangelo were gay. Apparently they were an item at one time and Michelangelo painted a few pictures of them together."

"Gay porn Michelangelos?" Hank asked.

"Not exactly," Villain replied. "Let's go take a look at them."

Villain led them into the next room, in which hung three paintings that were, to Hank's trained eye, unmistakably the work of the great Michelangelo. They weren't pornographic, exactly, but they did display both men in all their naked glory. "Now here's the thing," Villain said. "Take a close look at their naked buttocks."

"Do I have to?" Hank complained. Nevertheless he leaned in for a close look. On all the paintings both men clearly had distinctive moles in exactly the same location on their left buttocks.

"If this theory is right," Villain concluded, "both men were aliens, which might explain how both men were so far ahead of their times."

"But if they were trying to keep it a secret, why would Da Vinci reveal all of this in his notebooks?" Saphie asked.

"That's not completely clear," Villain confessed. "Maybe he just didn't think we could figure it out. Or he didn't care. My personal theory is that these aliens are tricksters. He just did it for fun."

"After the Renaissance, there's no further clue of the location of the aliens," Villain continued. "Except for one thing…"

"What's that?" Saphie asked excitedly.

"Hank, do you have a dollar bill on you?" Villain asked.

"Certainly."

"Take one out."

Hank pulled out his wallet. Ruffling through a thick wad of hundred- and thousand-dollar bills, he finally found a one-dollar bill. He pulled it out.

"Examine the back," Villain requested. "Has it ever occurred to you to wonder why there is a pyramid on the back of the United States one-dollar bill?"

"That is sort of strange," Hank admitted.

"The pyramid is the closest thing we have to the symbol for these aliens. The all-seeing eye above the pyramids symbolizes God. This seal seems to indicate that the aliens recognize the power of God over them. The fact that it's put on the back of a one-dollar bill seems to indicate the aliens' willingness to merge with human society, to blend in."

"That seems a bit of a stretch," Saphie said.

"Perhaps. But consider the Latin phrase below the pyramid: *Novus Ordo Seclorum.*"

"That means "a new order for the ages," Hank explained.

"Yes, indicating that the aliens were starting a new order of things, assimilation instead of domination."

"Maybe," Hank said.

"But there's another meaning. Saphie...?"

"It's an anagram, Uncle Rich. *Cure Ovums Soon, Lord.*"

"What the hell does that mean?" Hank asked.

"The best theory we have is that the aliens are immortal but infertile. They seem to believe that their infertility is a punishment from God."

"Surely aliens advanced enough to get here from another star, aliens that are powerful enough to convince us that they are gods, are too advanced to believe in God themselves. The whole thing seems very far-fetched," Hank complained.

"Perhaps. Certainly I won't try to convince you that God exists."

"Thanks for that, anyway," Hank said. "Besides, how could the aliens possibly sneak a message onto our one-dollar bill?"

"The great seal was designed in the late eighteenth century by the secretary of the Congress, Charles Thomson and Philadelphian William Barton. Both were Freemasons, as were George Washington, Benjamin Franklin and Thomas Jefferson," Villain explained.

Saphie took a deep breath. "Let me guess. The Masons were a cover for the aliens."

"Pop again, Saphie, that's right."

"Wait a minute. Grandfather was Grand Pubah of the Masons, and he was referring to some sort of alien weapon. Do you think he stumbled onto something that got him killed?" Saphie asked.

"It's possible, Saphie, I really don't know. I've made it my life's work to know everything there is to know about these aliens. But I don't know what happened to your grandfather. I suggest we table this conversation for now. We've got a big day tomorrow."

NINETEEN

Five hours of shoveling camel crap did little to improve the Poodle's mood. But after that disgusting chore was over they were able to sneak away and soon they were concealed in the stables, listening devices in position. He had missed most of their conversation, but he heard enough to know that Thomas would be heading for the Great Pyramid, and that it was critical that they learned what was found.

The Poodle and his men left Pemberley and entered the car, which they had left just outside the grounds. The Poodle dialed a number. "bin Laden," he said, "I need your help."

TWENTY

True to his word, Villain made arrangements for the foursome to obtain private access to the Great Pyramid. Impressive from far away, the Great Pyramid was intimidatingly huge as they got close.

Waiting to greet them was Sammy "Big Nose" bin Laden, Egypt's Minister of Culture. He was a large, jovial fellow who spoke perfect English.

"Saphie, Hank, let me introduce you to my good friend Sammy bin Laden. He was kind enough to make arrangements for us to visit the Subterranean Chamber. Sammy, this is Saphie Paradise, Eric's granddaughter, and the American art expert Hank Thomas. And of course you know my loyal dogsbody, Traitor McSneaky."

"Yes, of course. Pleased to meet you both," bin Laden declared. "Miss Paradise, I was a friend of your grandfather's. It was a great loss, a great loss. And Dr. Thomas, it's a pleasure to see you. You probably don't remember me, but I took your course in Phallic Symbology at Stanford when I was getting my master's."

"That explains your excellent English, Mr. bin Laden. You aren't by any chance related to..." Hank trailed off.

"Yes, yes, I am, and I bear the humiliation of it every day."

"I'm sorry for you," Hank said.

"You should be; it's not easy. With fifty brothers and sisters, it's really hard to make an impression, you know? And here I rise up to Minister of Culture and who has burst my bubble but little snot nose Osama. No sooner do I get this position than Osama becomes the great leader of a multi-national terrorist group. Big deal! I'm one of the top people in the Egyptian government; he lives in a cave, for Allah's sake. But who gets all of the press, all of the attention? The truth is," bin Laden confided, "Osama could care less about the Islamic revolution. He's just trying to one-up me in the eyes of Dad."

"Families are tough," Villain said sympathetically. "But we really need to get moving."

"No problem," bin Laden replied. "Just go into that Descending Passage and you'll run right into the Subterranean Chamber. Good luck."

The entrance to the Descending Passage started about five feet above ground level on the Great Pyramid. It consisted of a narrow shaft less than four feet high and slightly over three feet in width. They flipped on their headlamps and proceeded downward, first Hank, then Saphie, then Villain, and, finally, McSneaky.

The passage was tight and claustrophobic, and continued downward for three hundred feet. Finally, they arrived at the Subterranean Chamber. The chamber was small, perhaps six feet wide and twenty feet long. Thirty feet below the surface, the limestone room was dank and oxygen deprived.

The four of them searched the chamber, but found nothing that could possibly be a clue. At the end of the chamber was another passage, barely wide enough for Saphie to fit through. It dead-ended after five feet and provided no hint of a clue.

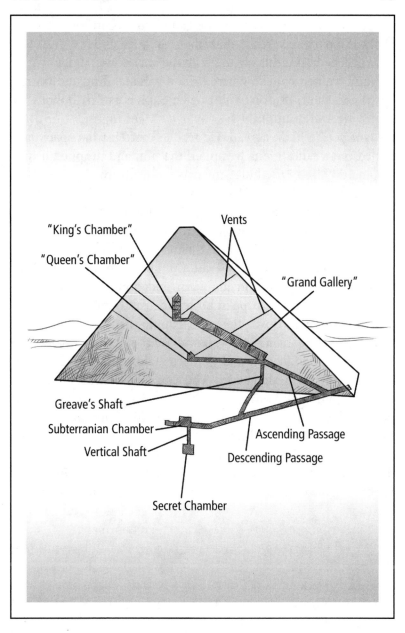

They continued to search the chamber. Villain looked curiously at a narrow vertical shaft that extended about eleven feet down. "The haiku did say to go all the way down, didn't it?"

Hank walked over to where Villain was standing and peered down the shaft. "I don't think even Saphie can fit down that shaft," he said doubtfully.

"Not yet," Villain agreed. He reached into his backpack and pulled out a hand grenade, pulled the pin, and dropped it into the shaft. "Fire in the hole!" he called cheerfully.

"Are we allowed..." Hank started to ask, but he was interrupted by a loud explosion. The whole room seemed to shake, and when they looked down the shaft was not only wider, it seemed to drop down much farther, at least twenty-five feet.

"Traitor, let down a rope." Traitor pulled a rope from his pack, wrapped one end around his waist and dropped it down the shaft. Traitor held the rope in both hands and braced himself as Villain scampered down the rope. Saphie turned to follow but Hank caught her arm. "Are you sure that's safe?" he asked.

Saphie smiled at him and grabbed hold of the rope. "If you can't trust Traitor McSneaky, who can you trust?" she asked, following Villain downward.

Hank looked doubtful, but grabbed hold of the rope and followed her down. The three of them found themselves in a cubical room roughly ten feet in dimension. In the center of the room was a stone table. On the table was a letter. "This is it," Saphie cried excitedly.

TWENTY-ONE

The letter consisted of one typed sentence.

```
Eric San Leté
Grand Pubah
The Ancient Order of the Masons

HITHERTO SHALT THOU COME, BUT NO FURTHER

Eric
```

Saphie looked at the letter in amazement. "What does it mean?"

Hank sighed heavily. "It means I screwed up. I got the haiku wrong. Is that all it says?"

Saphie flipped the letter over. There was some writing hastily scrawled on the back.

"You can kiss my ass, Karl!"

Villain looked forlornly at the letter. "So that's it, we're stuck?"

Saphie stood quietly, in deep contemplation. "Hank, read the haiku again."

Hank complied:

"Find four with three sides
And one with four…the tallest
Go all the way down."

Saphie smiled. "I've got it! We've been had! The true location is thousands of miles from here. I know exactly where to go."

TWENTY-TWO

The Poodle sat comfortably with his men in bin Laden's office, listening to every word that was spoken.

"I'm not happy about this," bin Laden complained. "Sir Richard is a friend of mine."

McGruff glared at bin Laden. "You'll do what we say, and like it. There's a shoot to kill out on you, Osama."

"That's my brother, and you know it. You can't shoot me!"

"Oh really. I'm a New York City police detective. What do you think the penalty would be if I shot the wrong bin Laden?"

"A fine?" bin Laden ventured.

"Ha! I'd probably get a medal. Anyway, you can stop fussing, because I've got what I need."

McGruff got on the phone to Rove and relayed the events in the Great Pyramid. Rove listened carefully, then said, "Okay, McGruff, I know where they are going. Here's what you need to do..."

TWENTY-THREE

The foursome made their way to the airport and booked the first passage back to the States. Hank had a little trepidation in going through Customs, but encountered no problems. Soon they were all comfortably ensconced into their first class seats, headed for New York. Hank, who had promised Saphie he would not say anything that could provoke divine retribution, was engrossed in the final chapters of *The Da Vinci Code*. Looking around the cabin, Saphie quickly realized that everyone was reading *The Da Vinci Code*. Apparently it was some sort of required reading in the U.S.

Hank closed his book with a sense of great satisfaction. "Now that is a great book," he murmured contentedly.

"May I?" Saphie asked.

Hank handed the book to Saphie, then rolled his eyes as he watched her literally flip through the pages. After a few minutes she handed the book back to him.

"You aren't going to pretend you just read that book, are you?" Hank demanded.

"Of course I did," Saphie said placidly. "You know I have an IQ of 215. But that book made no sense."

"Well, maybe you need to read it a little more carefully," Hank said. "It's a very complicated book."

"Maybe I did read it too fast. My understanding is that the plot hinges on Jacques Saunière's death. He's got a two-thousand-year-old secret, and if he dies the secret will be lost forever. In desperation he writes a code that will lead his granddaughter to the secret, so it won't be lost forever."

"You've got that much right," Hank conceded.

"But doesn't his wife, Marie Chauvel, also know the secret? So it isn't lost at all with his death, is it? And don't they plan on keeping the secret forever? So why the panic about the secret being lost if they intend to never reveal it anyway?" Saphie asked.

"Well, you see..." Hank began.

"And Sophie is a sophisticated Parisian woman who is horrified out of her mind by the sight of her grandfather having sex? And since the final revelation is in the Louvre, yards from where Saunière dies, he couldn't think of an easier way of leading Sophie to it? And by the way, apparently Robert Langdon and Leigh Teabing both know the secret of the Holy Grail already. So how secret is this secret?"

"Well," Hank tried, "the key is finding the actual descendants of Christ. That's the real secret."

"That's nonsense. If Jesus had borne children, those children have been having children of their own for 2,000 years. The mathematics of reproduction dictates that a huge percentage, probably most, of the human race would be descended from Jesus by now."

"That can't be right."

"Oh yes, it is. Scientists estimate that virtually everyone living in Britain today is a descendant of everyone who lived in Britain in the year 1000 A.D., assuming that a person from 1000 A.D. has any living descendants at all. And that was only 1,000 years ago.

Someone from the time of Jesus, if he has any descendants living to the present day, would have hundreds of millions of descendants. So being a direct descendant of Jesus would be no big deal at all."

"But it has all these cool puzzles," Hank protested. "Does it really have to make sense?"

"Of course not," Saphie conceded.

TWENTY-FOUR

The next day they were at their final destination, Saphie leading the way, followed by Villain and Hank. Mc-Sneaky waited in their rented limousine outside.

They entered the giant pyramid, looking for a way to the bottom. Saphie pushed the button for the elevator, headed down. The elevator opened and they stepped in. The elevator panel read "Enter Key for Lower Levels."

"The pastrami key!" Hank said excitedly.

Saphie removed the pastrami key from around her neck. She put the key into the panel slot and turned it. A panel slid open, revealing a new set of buttons. The bottom button read "All the Way Down." Saphie pushed it.

The elevator fell so sharply they almost stumbled. After a good five minutes, the elevator finally slowed to a stop.

The elevator door opened.

They walked into a large circular room. The walls, floors and ceiling were a deep, non-reflective black. The walls curved in a three-hundred-and-sixty-degree circle that was only broken in three places: by the elevator door and by two doors that lay ahead of them. The first door was clearly labeled "A"; the second door was labeled "B." In front of each door stood a short, but evil-looking robot that seemed to be guarding the door. Squat and circular, bristling with sharp edges, these robots looked like sadistic R2D2s.

"Oh, no," Villain cried.

"What are they?" Saphie asked.

"I've never seen these before, but I know what they are. Those are alien robot guards, which means we're in an alien logic maze. This is hopeless."

"Calm down, Uncle Rich. Will those robots let us pass?"

"They'll let us pass, all right. But only one of those doors leads to the weapon. The other one leads to an incinerator. Those robots will lock the door behind us. If we choose the wrong door we're good as dead. It's hopeless. If we don't know the right pattern of doors, we'll never get through this maze."

Hank was examining the robots, which were perfectly still. "Do these things talk? Maybe we can just ask them which door is right."

"The aliens aren't dumb, Hank. The robots talk, but there's no way of knowing whether they are telling the truth, because there are two models of robot. The model Ts always tell the truth and the model Fs always lie. But they always put one of each pair together so there's no way to know who is lying and who isn't."

"This will be easy," Hank exclaimed. He turned to the first robot. "Do you lie?" he asked.

"Of course not," the robot intoned, sounding offended.

"Great," Hank concluded. "This one must be Model T…unless it's model F."

"Let me try," Saphie suggested. She approached the robot in front of the B door. Pointing to the A robot, she asked, "Is he a model T?"

"Yes," the robot replied.

"That means…" Saphie began.

"Oh wait, I forgot something. My research revealed that due to a programming glitch the Model Ts lie in the morning, and the Model Fs tell the truth in the morning. It's a bit confusing," Villain said apologetically.

"Well, what time is it?" Hank asked. None of them knew; it was around lunchtime, but they weren't sure if it was technically morning or afternoon.

"It's morning," Robot A chimed in.

"He's right," Saphie agreed. She turned to Robot B. "Is the alien weapon behind your door?"

"Yup," Robot B agreed.

"He's lying," Saphie declared, marching through the door marked A.

The next room was identical to the first.

"Which one of you is Model F?" Saphie asked.

"We both are," declared the robot in front of Door A.

"He isn't," stated the robot in front of Door B, pointing at Robot A.

"Does your door have the alien weapon?" Saphie asked Robot B.

"Of course," he replied and Saphie marched through Door B, the others trailing behind her.

The next room had three doors, labeled A, B and C, and a robot in front of each. "Now what?" Hank cried.

"I'm pretty sure there are more model Fs than model Ts. It's pretty safe to assume that only one of these is a model T," Villain said.

"Well, which of you is the model T?" Hank asked plaintively.

"B is," Robot A said.

"A is," Robot C said.

Saphie looked at Robot B. "What do you have to say for yourself?"

"I can tell you for sure that Robot C is a model F," Robot B said smugly.

"It's still morning," Saphie said confidently. She turned to Robot A. "Is the alien weapon past your door?"

"It sure isn't," he replied.

"Liar," said Saphie as she marched through Door A, the others trailing behind her.

The next room was identical. Three robots stood in front of three doors.

"Is it still morning?" Hank wondered aloud.

"I'm not saying," Robot A said slyly. "Ask B; he would tell you it's morning."

"So would C," Robot B said defensively.

"Speak for yourself," intoned Robot C. "A would say it was afternoon, I'll tell you that."

"It is afternoon now," Saphie declared. "B is telling the truth." She looked at B. "Which door?" she asked.

"Door C," B said forlornly.

They walked through Door C. The room they entered was round, like the others, but entirely white. At the far end of the room was an elevator door. At the center was a table. On it lay a plain white envelope.

"Another clue," Hank groaned.

Saphie walked up to the envelope and examined it. It was clearly labeled, "WMD."

TWENTY-FIVE

aphie walked up to the envelope with some trepidation. *What sort of weapon could this be?* She carefully picked up the envelope and started to open it.

"I'd wait with that," Villain warned. "We don't know what that is. Let's get it out of here where we can carefully examine it."

"We can go to my place in Palo Alto," Hank offered. "It's not all that far from here."

Saphie clutched the envelope to her chest and headed for the elevator door. The elevator rose for a good ten minutes before opening. They were in the lobby. Everything looked surprisingly, shockingly normal.

But as they left the building they were surrounded by the Poodle's men. McGruff walked up to them, a big smile on his face. "Well, well, well, what have we here? You three are in quite a bit of trouble. You can start by handing me the alien weapon, whatever that is."

Saphie froze, startled. She tried to hold the envelope casually, hoping McGruff wouldn't notice. *We are so close...Grandfather, I'm sorry...*

Hank unobtrusively balled his right hand into a fist and shoved it into his jacket pocket. He waved his pocket around threateningly. "Hold it, McGruff. I will use this weapon if I have to. I'm not sure how much of this city it will take out."

"You're bluffing, Thomas. You use that weapon and you're as good as dead."

Hank looked McGruff straight in the eye. "Try me."

Just then McGruff's phone rang. Keeping his eyes on Thomas, he answered it. "Yes?"

"This is Rove. Let them go. You can't risk a deployment of the weapon, not without knowing what it is. Let them go but follow them. I'm coming to deal with this personally."

"But, Mr. Rove..."

"Just do as I say, McGruff. Karl knows best."

McGruff hung up the phone. He glared at Hank. "Fine, you can go. But when I get my hands on you..."

Hank, Saphie and Villain quickly raced to the curb and got into their waiting limousine, McSneaky at the wheel.

"Hank, you were brilliant!" Saphie exclaimed.

Hank felt dizzy. He gave her a reassuring smile. "Well, you know..."

TWENTY-SIX

They soon arrived at Hank's home in Palo Alto. It was not so much of a house as a palace, built in French Renaissance style. McSneaky pulled the limo up to the grand entrance and the four of them entered. Villain looked around, trying not to seem too impressed. "A bit showy, isn't it? You make Trump seem low key," Villain ventured.

"Look who's talking, Mr. Pemberley with slaves," Hank retorted.

"Enough, guys," Saphie interjected. "It's time to open this thing." They were all standing around Saphie in Hank's large and elaborately furnished drawing room. She carefully pulled open the envelope. Inside was a sheet of paper. Saphie began to read.

The Universe

Human physicists, whose efforts we have always held in such contempt, have discovered much about the universe. While our technology is well beyond theirs, their theoretical knowledge of the universe is unparalleled. I've made it my business to keep up with their developments and I have come to the realization that humans have stumbled onto a secret that we, for all of our knowledge, have missed.

A secret of such profundity and inspiration that I shake with joy and amazement even as I think of it.

Much of the universe is explained by theory. We understand how gravity works, how electromagnetic forces interact, the curious behaviors of the subatomic. We understand how all of these work together. Our theories all fit together and make sense as a whole. You can't randomly fiddle with one part of the theory or the whole structure falls apart. This is what gives us the confidence that our models of the universe approximate truth. They hold together and are consistent. They are deliberate, not random.

But there are a few things that we do not learn from theory; these are the cosmological constants. The power of the force of gravity, or of the strong nuclear force, the mass of an electron or the universe itself, the speed of light or the rate of proton decay; these are all cosmological constants. Theory doesn't tell us what these should be. We observe the numbers and we plug them into our theories.

As far as our theories are concerned, these constants could be anything. They could change at will and our theories would still work, but the outcomes for the nature of our universe would be dramatically different.

The fundamental truth the humans have stumbled onto is this. The cosmological constants are not random at all; they were chosen, very precisely, to achieve a very specific goal.

They were chosen to allow us to live.

The evidence is overwhelming. If the force of gravity were only slightly stronger, stars would be more massive, but they would burn too rapidly and unevenly to support life. Our race could not exist. If the force of gravity were slightly weaker, stars would not be large enough to generate the heavy elements needed for life to develop. Again, we would not exist.

If the strong nuclear force, which holds together the particles in the nucleus of an atom, were slightly weaker, the universe would consist entirely of hydrogen. If the force were slightly stronger, there would be virtually no hydrogen, and therefore no stars. Either way, we would not exist.

If the weak nuclear force were slightly weaker, neutrons would decay much faster, and little helium would have been produced in the big bang, meaning no heavy elements allowing life. If the force were slightly stronger, all of the hydrogen would have become helium in the big bang, and therefore, again, no stars. Either way, we would not exist.

If the electromagnetic force, which binds electrons to protons in atoms were slightly stronger, atoms could not form into molecules. If it were slightly weaker, electrons would fly away from atoms, and atoms would not be stable. Either way, we would not exist.

If the ratio of proton to electron mass were slightly different, again, molecules would not form. We could not exist.

If the expansion of the universe were slightly slower, the universe would have collapsed before stars had a chance to form. If the universe were expanding more quickly, no galaxies and there-fore no stars would ever form. The expansion rate must be fine-tuned to an incredibly precise rate, accurate to one part in 10^{55}. If not, we could not exist.

The entropy level, mass and uniformity of the universe all must be carefully fine-tuned, or we could not exist.

The stability of the proton, the fine structure constants of the fundamental forces, the velocity of light, the energy levels of oxygen, carbon and beryllium, the luminosity of stars, the distance between stars, all of these measures, all of which could be almost anything, are exactly what we need to live. Vary any one of them, even a little, and we could not exist.

The evidence is undeniable. Someone designed this universe, and designed it for us.

God has turned Her back on us. She has cursed us, even. But She still exists, and we must now all accept that undeniable fact.

Our faith has been sorely tried, but our faith is no longer need-ed. We have proof of God. It's time we devoted ourselves to pleasing Her.

This war must end.

Hank and Saphie looked at each other in amazement. *Can this really be proof of God?* Hank thought. *How is this a weapon?* Saphie wondered.

They turned to look at Villain. He was on his knees, weep-ing openly. "God, we have forsaken you," he cried between his sobs. "God is real; I knew, but I did not really believe."

Villain pulled himself together. He stood up and faced Saphie and Hank. "This changes everything," Villain declared. "The war is over, and we have won. I can't believe it. Eric is a genius. Thank you, Lord."

Saphie looked at Villain in puzzlement. "I don't understand, Uncle Rich. What war? How is this a weapon? What's going on?"

Villain looked at Saphie affectionately, his eyes gleaming with tears. "There's no reason to hide anything from you anymore. I'll tell you everything, but not tonight. I need some time to recover from this shock. Let's get some sleep, and in the morning I'll answer all of your questions."

TWENTY-SEVEN

Hank and Saphie walked slowly up the broad spiral staircase that led to their rooms. Their minds buzzed with the seemingly unbelievable information they had been given. *Proof of God*, Hank thought. *Alien religious wars...it's all so crazy.*

Saphie followed Hank into his room and dropped heavily into a rare Louis IV settee. "Are you buying all this? Aliens battling over the existence of God?"

"I don't know, Saphie. It seems quite unbelievable. Do you trust Villain?"

"My grandfather did. I wish he were still here. I wish I had..." Saphie began to cry quietly. She thought of the letters he had sent her, which she had burned unread.

Hank joined her on the settee and put his arm around her shoulders and gently pulled her toward his chest. Her sobbing grew and Hank began patting his pockets for a handkerchief. *I wish she would stop crying*, he reflected. *This suit is Armani.*

"Saphie, what did happen between you and your grandfather?" Hank finally asked. "What did he do that was so horrible?"

Saphie got up and walked into the bathroom. When she

emerged, her tears were gone and she gave Hank a faint smile. She sat back down next to him. "I've never told anyone this," she admitted. "But I need to know…did I overreact?"

As she began to recount what had happened that night, she felt herself drifting back to four years earlier. It was her first month as a freshman at Harvard, and she was homesick. It was mid-September, a time when she always felt Paris was at its most beautiful. She decided to head back to Paris for the weekend and surprise her grandfather. When he was not to be found in their Paris apartment, she headed for her grandfather's chateau in the Parisian suburbs. She was so excited on the drive. *How I miss my grandfather*, she thought. Those lovable Parisian street kids were up to their usual shenanigans, and all around her shops and cars were aflame, almost as if celebrating her return home.

When she got to the chateau she quietly let herself in, determined to surprise her grandfather. When she opened the door, she immediately heard the sound of drums and chanting. *Is grandfather up to another of his "religious" mass orgies? That guy really needs to keep it in his pants*, she thought affectionately.

But no, her grandfather was by himself, sitting quietly at the dining room table having an early meal. He was wearing his old patched green sweater, white linen pants and white shoes. She drew closer and was consumed with horror. For a few quiet moments she only stood staring at her grandfather, gasping for breath. Then she began to scream…

"Saphie, calm down, please," Hank said. "I agree, it was quite horrible. Are you completely sure that he was wearing white shoes after Labor Day? And linen pants as well…that is pretty bad."

"What?" Saphie asked, confused.

"Of course, many etiquette advisors are suggesting that wear-

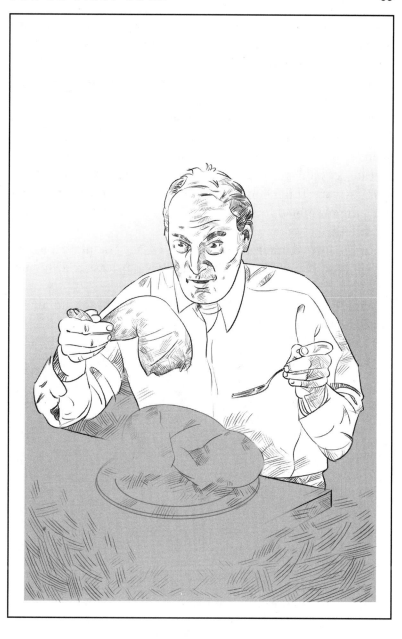

ing white shoes after Labor Day isn't as big a faux pas as it once was. Bad taste, I'll grant you. But still, your reaction might have been a wee bit extreme."

"I'm not done yet, Hank," Saphie said testily. Again, she flowed back into that horrible time, as if she were reliving it.

On the dining room table was a large platter containing what could only be a roasted human baby, along with a bowl of fava beans and a nice Chianti. Her grandfather was a cannibal! And an eater of babies at that! San Leté turned with a start with Saphie's scream, thigh bone still in his hand. "It's not what it looks like," he mumbled, his mouth still full of exquisitely prepared baby flesh.

Saphie turned and ran. She never saw her grandfather again.

"Hank, did I overreact? Should I have at least read his letters?"

Hank couldn't answer. He was noisily vomiting into an antique Louis XVI wastepaper basket.

TWENTY-EIGHT

Hank cleaned himself up and returned to his room. He sat quietly next to Saphie for a few minutes. Finally, he broke the silence. "Maybe we should get some sleep," he suggested gently, his face lowered.

Saphie turned toward Hank and put her palms on his cheeks. She turned his head toward hers. "I'm not a lesbian."

"Well, symbologically speaking..." Hank started, but Saphie interrupted his speech with a quick but passionate kiss.

"I'm not a lesbian," Saphie repeated, "and I'm prepared to prove it." She kissed him again, longer this time.

Hank was in shock. For all his wealth, experience, savoir faire and deep understanding of symbology, Hank had never actually had sex with a woman before. He wasn't quite sure what to do next.

Fortunately, Saphie knew exactly what to do. She pulled him toward the bed, and began slowly removing his clothes.

Seventeen minutes later, Hank Thomas entered Paradise.

TWENTY-NINE

Snap!
Snap!
Snap!
The whip cut cruelly into Rove's back and buttocks. He no longer believed in God, but some of the ancient rituals still had power. Mortification of the flesh cleansed the soul before battle. And battle was coming.

Pain is good, Rove thought.

Snap!
Snap!
Snap!

He would have cried out, but the ball gag kept his cries from leaving his throat. His face was encased by a leather mask, and his ankles were tightly tied.

"Has my piggy wiggy had enough?" the dominatrix asked cruelly. "Crawl over here and lick my toes."

Rove crawled awkwardly to the feet of his Mistress, his bound ankles making slow work of it.

Pain is good, he thought as he licked.

THIRTY

Hank woke up with a smile on his face. He had never felt this good before; he just wanted to laugh. This must be what love felt like. And he did love Saphie, from her cute button nose to her tiny toes, from her small but ample breasts to the tiny mole on her buttocks…

"Hmmm," Hank thought.

Saphie was waking up. "Good morning, Hank," she said with a shy smile. "How are you feeling?"

"I always feel great when I'm with you, Saphie," Hank said. "Last night was wonderful."

"For me too, Hank. Now, you ready to hear Uncle Rich's story?"

"As ready as I'll ever be."

They quickly dressed and went downstairs. McSneaky was in the kitchen, preparing breakfast. "I took the liberty of having Traitor prepare our breakfast," Villain said. "I hope that's all right."

"Of course, Sir Richard. My house is your house," Hank said graciously.

As they sat down to breakfast they heard a crash and turned to see a man jumping through the large plate glass windows of Hank's living room. The man hit the ground, rolled, and stood in one smooth motion. It was Karl Rove, and in his hands was a lethal-looking automatic.

"No one move," Rove said calmly. "I'm taking the weapon."

Hank shoved his hand into his jacket pocket and waved it around. "Drop the gun or I'll deploy the alien weapon."

Rove looked at Hank contemptuously. "That trick only works once, moron."

But his eyes were drawn to Hank, and as they were, Villain made his move. Almost faster than the eye could see, his hand swept into Rove's, knocking his gun across the room. Soon the men were wrestling frantically on the ground.

Hank and Saphie watched in frozen fascination as the two men wrestled. As they struggled their clothes ripped apart and each man seemed to grow an additional pair of arms and legs. Soon they rolled, naked, on the ground, each man's eight limbs struggling with the other's. Hank couldn't help but notice both men had distinctive moles on their left buttocks.

Saphie recovered first and grabbed the first heavy object she could find—a Louis XII chamber pot—and brained Rove with it. He jerked and fell unconscious. As they watched, his extra limbs retracted and disappeared. As Villain stood, breathing heavily, his did the same.

"You're both aliens!" Saphie cried.

"Yes." Villain admitted. "As is Eric San Leté."

"What? That's impossible."

"Honestly, Saphie, I thought you knew, or at least suspected. Eric San Leté is an anagram for *secret alien*. It's not even a hard one."

Hank began to giggle. "Eric San Leté, *secret alien*. It's an easy one. How long have you lived with San Leté? I thought you were the anagram master! An IQ of 215...how did you miss that one?" Hank continued to giggle.

"Oh, shut up, Hank," Saphie ordered miserably.

"When your parents died Eric adopted you as an experiment in human childrearing. Thetans—that's the name of our race—can't have children. We've been sterile for millions of years," Villain explained.

"I promised you both the truth and you'll get it," Villain continued. "Just let me get some clothes on. Is it okay if I borrow something of yours, Hank?"

"Sure," Hank said, dazed and trying to hold back his giggles.

"I'll be right back. You should tie him up."

Saphie and Hank tied Rove's hands and feet together. How much good this would do if he grew more limbs they couldn't say. Hank looked around the room. "What happened to the gun?" he asked.

Saphie frowned. "I don't see it."

Soon Villain was back and they sat down at the breakfast table. McSneaky served them coffee as they talked.

"There's a lot to tell you," Villain began. "I'm not sure where to start."

"Why don't you start at the beginning?" Saphie suggested.

"All right, I will. Approximately twenty-five million years ago, a group of a few hundred of us Thetans arrived on Earth. We were the last remnants of a thriving civilization of millions that was lost when our sun was destroyed. Our technology was well beyond that of yours today, but not enormously so; but we were able to build one star-spanning craft, and over thousands of years of searching it ultimately made its way to Earth.

"We were always a very religious people, but our faith was shaken by the destruction of our home world. This was known as the First Spiritual Crisis. We overcame this crisis by deciding that we had come to this planet, Earth, for a reason. That we were destined to do some great good here.

"We found your monkey-like ancestors and decided, despite their shortage of limbs, that they had the potential for sentience. You have to remember that we were very lonely, and we needed a mission—something to give us purpose. For millions of years, that purpose was humanity. We played with your genes, controlled your evolution, did what we needed to do to help you evolve into modern humans.

"At the same time we modified ourselves so we could blend into humanity. Through genetic engineering we reduced the number of our limbs from eight to four—the other four only emerge in times of stress—and made other cosmetic changes to allow ourselves to fit in."

"Da Vinci's *Vitruvian Man!*" Hank interjected.

"That's right, Hank," Villain responded. "I told you Da Vinci was a joker. His *Vitruvian Man* was nothing less than an accurate portrayal of the original Thetan form."

"But there was a problem. Tinkering with our genetic code had left us sterile. We are an extremely long-lived race, effectively immortal, but now we could not have children. Without children our lives were empty; our civilization pointless. We reproduce by budding—the mole on our buttocks is a bud, which ultimately becomes a child. But now these moles just serve as reminders of what we lost."

"So, Uncle Rich, if I should still call you that, Thetans are asexual?"

"Not exactly, Saphie. We do have sex and we co-mingle genetic material. But either gender can bear children. The genetic co-mingling goes on in our 'life center,' located in the large intestine. The merged genetic code moves to our 'mole,' which grows to about the size of a grape. Then it drops off, we put it in a crib, and a week later we have a squalling infant baby. It's a lot better than your method, which, frankly, is quite grotesque."

"So all of the UFO sightings, over the years, that was you Thetans?" Hank asked.

"Yes, Hank."

"And the kidnappings, the reports of anal probings...was that you as well?"

"Remember, Hank, that we were—we are—desperate to find a solution to our infertility. We investigated the life centers of humans, or tried to. By the 1950s we concluded that humans have no life centers, only Thetans do. You have to understand, Hank, that we did this research in desperation; it's not like we did anal probings for the fun of it."

"By the 1950s you were convinced that humans didn't have life centers, right? Then why did reports of anal probings continue into the 1980s?"

"Well," Villain said apologetically, "we mostly didn't do it for fun. But it was pretty funny!

"The point is that our infertility hurt us deeply; this became our Second Spiritual Crisis. Again, we took heart in humanity. Humans would be our children.

"Once mankind was evolved enough for civilization, we set ourselves up as ruler-gods, in Egypt, Sumeria and countless other places. But mankind was not so easily dominated and people rebelled against us.

"We decided that you were growing up and a lighter hand was needed. We decided to guide humanity via the auspices of the Catholic Church. Again, people rebelled and Christianity was splintered into many sects. We lost control.

"This led to the Third Spiritual Crisis, which split our race into two camps. Some took these failures as an indication that our attempts to dominate were hubris, and God wanted them to live among the humans, but not as rulers. This camp, the Theists, chose lifestyles that immersed themselves into the human population, and spent lives devoted to art and science.

"But the other camp lost heart. They took these failures as signs that their exile was meaningless, that God was dead, and that they should continue their attempts to rule man, but not as benevolent elder brothers, but for power's own sake.

"The Theists formed the Freemasons as a platform for peacefully integrating into humanity. I am a Freemason, as is your grandfather. So were Da Vinci and Michelangelo. And, I should add for Hank's benefit, so was Jackson Pollock. By the way, Hank, good show on unraveling the nineteenth level. We had a pool going on how long it would take before a human figured it out."

"Thank you," Hank replied.

"Later, the Atheists organized into the Scientologists in yet another attempt to dominate humanity through mind control. Each group kept a wary eye on the others. The Atheists were forced to low key their efforts at domination, for fear of the Theists. And the Theists never abandoned their efforts to convince the Atheists they were on the wrong path. It was a stalemate."

"Your 'grandfather' came up with a weapon that would end this stalemate; I had no idea what it was until yesterday, and the truth was better than anything I could have imagined. He is truly a brilliant man. A definitive, incontrovertible proof of the existence of God. This will knock the wind out of the sails of the Atheists for sure. They'll be forced to acknowledge they were wrong."

Saphie suddenly realized something. "Why are you referring to grandfather in the present tense?"

Villain smiled. "Eric isn't dead, Saphie. We Thetans are tough to kill, and no Thetan would ever kill another, not even an atheist like Rove. But what happened to him is very serious. Thetans are most vulnerable in their life centers. I'm afraid that Rove provided a direct electrical stimulation to Eric's life center. He may have managed to stay awake for a few minutes, but he was soon forced into a death-like hibernation."

"That explains the mess," observed Hank.

"How long before he awakes?" Saphie asked desperately.

"I'm sorry, Saphie. Eric won't recover for thousands of years. You'll be long dead before he's up and around again."

THIRTY-ONE

Villain spoke quickly. "We need to head to Washington D.C., and confront W with the proof of God's existence. With a little luck he'll agree to join the Theists and abandon his attempts to dominate mankind."

Hank looked dubious. "Will this news really make that much of a difference?"

Villain looked quite certain. "Oh yes, you have to remember how big a deal it is for a Thetan to lose faith in God. We are religious by nature, and only the most grievous of disappointments could drive us—some of us—to atheism. W and his group are hardcore, no doubt. But faced with incontrovertible proof of God's existence, he will welcome it. We need to head to the Founding Church of Scientology in D.C. That's our best shot at catching W off guard."

Saphie looked puzzled. "So the Scientologists are aliens?"

"No. Most of the Scientologists," Villain explained, "are innocent dupes. But the leadership is composed of the heads of the Thetan atheist clique. The Founding Church of Scientology is their power center and the place where W spends his considerable 'vacation' time. It's ironic that much of the public considers him a layabout," Villain explained. "W's actually the hardest-working Thetan I've ever met. It's just that being President is the least of his responsibilities."

"But I thought W was in Crawford, Texas. That's where his vacation home is," Hank interjected.

"That's actually a common misconception," Villain explained.

Hank frowned and Saphie gave him a sharp look and a wink. "It's irritating, isn't it?" she whispered sweetly.

"Do you really think the most powerful man on the planet spends his free time clearing brush? Does that seem remotely credible to you?"

"Well, no."

"Reagan started that; he was a hell of a joker. And then it sort of became a running joke."

"So all the Presidents have been aliens?" Hank asked in amazement.

"Oh, no," Villain responded. "Clinton was human. The whole Monica thing was a dead giveaway. We Thetans aren't above sleeping with interns, certainly. But Monica? After a few million years of life, one develops a little taste. Marilyn Monroe, yes. Monica, no way."

"So are you saying that Kennedy...?"

Villain gave him a broad wink. "What do you think?"

T H I R T Y - T W O

They were soon on Hank's private jet, headed to Washington D.C. McSneaky, who, fortunately, was a licensed pilot, flew the plane, while the other four—Hank, Saphie, Villain and a bound and unconscious Rove— were in the cabin. Villain looked around the cabin. "We need some way of taking Rove with us. W will want to know what's become of him."

Hank opened a hatch leading down to the pressurized storage area. "I've got a large trunk," he offered, "but we'll have to empty it."

Hank and Saphie went below and Hank opened the trunk. It was filled with $100 bills. "Getaway money?" Saphie inquired.

"Not really," Hank replied. "I'm just running out of places to put the stuff."

They dragged the now-empty trunk up to the main cabin. It was a tight fit, but they got the unconscious figure of Rove into the trunk and sealed it shut. Rove stirred, but did not wake up. Upon landing they loaded the trunk into the trunk of the waiting limousine and drove off.

They were headed for Fraser Mansion, home of the Founding Church of Scientology, located at R Street and Connecticut

Avenue, a few blocks from fashionable Dupont Circle. Taking its name from the man for whom it was built as a residence in 1890, George S. Fraser, this historical mansion was designed by architects Joseph Hornblower and James Marshall, renowned for their design of the Smithsonian Museum of Natural History, George Washington University's Law School, the Monkey House at the National Zoo, the Phillips Collection, and the Army and Navy Club building. L. Ron Hubbard had lived in Washington D.C. for many years, and, even more than the first Scientology Church in Los Angeles, the Founding Church in D.C. was considered "ground zero" of the Scientology Church.

They entered the church, Villain in the lead, followed by Saphie. Hank and McSneaky took the rear carrying the heavy trunk between them. The reception area was beautiful, with solid white oak flooring and elaborate wood carvings on the walls. At the reception desk stood a young, fresh-faced woman who greeted them cheerfully. "Are you here for your audits?"

"We've got a meeting in the chapel," Villain said unceremoniously as he charged by her. The other three followed. The chapel was quite beautiful, with comfortable leather chairs and an ornate set of stained glass windows behind the pulpit. Hank and McSneaky put down the trunk heavily. "He's usually in here somewhere," Villain muttered, racing to the front, Hank and Saphie following. But there was nothing.

"I guess we wait," Hank suggested.

"I have a better idea," McSneaky said. He was facing them holding Rove's fallen automatic. He had opened the trunk and Rove stood beside him, looking groggy.

"W will be very pleased with this catch," Rove stated with a smile.

"I can't believe you're a traitor, Traitor," Villain cried. "Why?"

"Maybe because you've treated me like crap for thirty years?"

Hank nodded sagely. Traitor McSneaky. It was obvious, in retrospect. He would never doubt symbolic analysis again.

"I'll take the weapon now," Rove demanded.

"Is this what you want, Rove?" Hank said, holding the envelope with the alien weapon. With a mighty throw, he flung it into the air.

Rove watched serenely as the envelope sailed through the air and landed in a corner of the room. He looked at Hank with a mixture of surprise and contempt. "You are an idiot, human," he said, laughing and walking to the corner of the room to pick up the envelope. But as his eyes were turned downward Hank leaped, and they were soon struggling for the gun. Just as Hank was gaining the upper hand he heard a voice boom, "FREEZE!"

Hank looked up. They were surrounded by Secret Service agents, standing with weapons drawn. Hank stood up, his hands in the air.

"I'll take that," Rove said, picking up the envelope. "Okay, everybody, you wanted to see W. Let's see him."

THIRTY-THREE

H ank, Saphie and Villain found themselves seated in a large white couch in the Oval Office. Across from them sat Karl Rove and sitting behind his desk was George W. Bush. The Secret Service agents were reluctant to leave, but once they had securely bound the three prisoners W insisted they leave. Hank inspected W closely. "I can't believe you're an alien."

W glared at Villain. "That was a secret you were never supposed to learn. I'm sorry you did."

"But why do you feel the need to dominate humanity? Why can't our races live together in peace?"

W gave a superior smirk. "Villain's been filling your head with nonsense. We ARE living in peace. This isn't about domination, not really. But we are stuck on this planet and all meaning and purpose has been stripped from our lives. We are immortals living in a Godless universe, surrounded by humans, our most foolish creation. Why not be in charge? Why not benefit from whatever feeble comforts humans have managed to create? What else would you suggest for us?"

"Fine," Saphie exclaimed. "Live your lives, be happy. But why do you need to run the world? And why shove all your right-wing principles down this country's throat?"

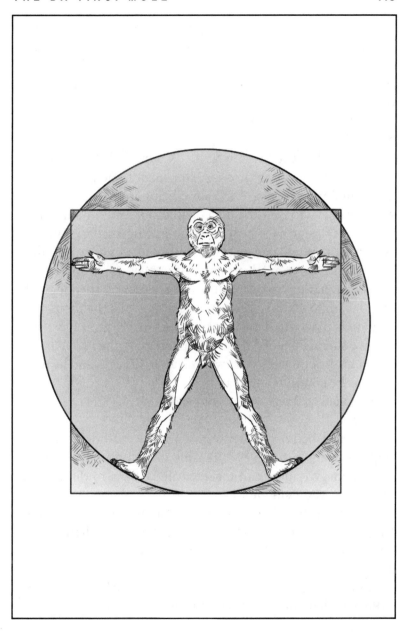

"These right-wing 'principles' are only a matter of self-preservation, Saphie," W explained. "We have to pretend to die every eighty years or so, so this death tax was a killer. We had to get rid of that. And lower taxes on the rich, well, we are all rich, you know."

"And all this religious nonsense that you pretend to believe..." Hank began.

"It's true that I've lost my faith," W admitted. "That loss was the most painful thing that has happened to me in a life spanning millions of years. Naturally I support religion; humans shouldn't have to bear the pain of atheism. And my support for intelligent design is simply because intelligent design is true. We were the intelligence; if not for us you would still be monkeys. Don't be so quick to judge us; we're doing the best we can for humanity in a very difficult situation. But enough chit chat. I want to see this weapon. Eric is no fool; if he thought the weapon is powerful, I'm sure it will be. Karl?"

Rove silently handed the envelope to W. W opened it and began to read. Soon tears were welling up in his eyes and he wiped them as he continued to read.

W looked at Rove. "Have you read this?"

"I have."

"I can't believe it; we were wrong. God does exist!" W laughed, tears in his eyes. "It's time to rethink our whole position here. We must call together all Thetans to discuss this. Karl, aren't you delighted?"

"Not really, W. Okay, God exists. But She has abandoned us. She has left us on this planet, sterile, without children or a real future. I'd rather there was no God than a God that would abandon us like this."

"You're wrong, Karl," W began.

Rove pulled out his revolver and pointed it at the threesome.

"Here's what we're going to do. We're going to kill these three, and then we are going to burn that letter. Nothing has to change."

"You are wrong about that," came a deep booming voice from behind them. Rove whirled to see Eric San Leté standing behind him. San Leté looked fit and much younger than when Saphie had seen him last. His voice, previously quiet and soft, was now a deep booming basso.

"You were supposed to be out for centuries, Eric," Rove said cruelly. "But I'm glad you're here. It saves me the trouble of digging you up and killing you."

"You know I'm a geneticist, Karl," San Leté said calmly. "I've done a lot of work on my life center. It's now much more resilient than the typical Thetan's."

Rove was unimpressed. "We'll see how it likes a bullet, Eric."

W looked miserable. "It's too late, Karl. God exists. We can't go on pretending She doesn't."

Rove whirled on W. "God abandoned us, W. I can't let that go so easily."

"She didn't, Karl," San Leté declared. "You're wrong about that. Our sterility was caused by our science and our hubris, and it can be cured with science and a little humility."

"Don't talk nonsense," Rove snapped. "In millions of years of trying no Thetan has ever borne a child."

San Leté looked directly at Saphie. "That's not exactly true."

Saphie gazed back at San Leté, tears welling up in her eyes.

"That's right, Saphie; you were never told what happened to your father," San Leté boomed.

"I know enough. I know he was killed in a car crash."

"No. I am your father," San Leté replied, his booming voice giving the statement an air of ominous truth.

"No. No. It's not true. That's impossible," Saphie screamed.

"Search your feelings, Saphie. You know it to be true."

"Noooo. Noooo," Saphie screamed these words.

"Aren't you overreacting a bit, Princess Saphie?" San Leté asked gently.

Saphie searched her feelings. She realized that at some level she'd always known that San Leté was her father. "I'm not your Princess Saphie anymore. You're a baby eater."

"Oh that. I tried to explain but you wouldn't listen. That was a puglunk; it's a Thetan delicacy. It does look a lot like a human baby," he admitted.

W nodded in agreement. "Good stuff. I could go for a puglunk sandwich right about now."

Rove still waved his gun. "We can eat later, after they are dead. Eric, Saphie may be a fool but I'm not. I don't believe your story for a second."

"Really?" San Leté responded. He turned his back on Rove, pulled down his pants, and bent over, mooning them all.

"That's a bit childish," Hank observed.

"No, Hank, look at his buttocks!" Saphie exclaimed.

"Do I have to?" Hank looked. Where San Leté's mole should have been was a bright pink spot.

"Oh my God," cried Rove.

"It's true! How did you do it?" W exclaimed.

"It wasn't easy, and there were some glitches. Saphie went through an unfortunate fish phase. But I think I have the kinks worked out. By next year, all of you could be budding like mad."

Rove dropped his gun and fell to his knees, openly weeping. "I'm so sorry, Eric. I never guessed..."

"It's okay now, Karl," San Leté said generously. "We're all one family now."

"Hey, wait a minute," Saphie said. "Does this mean I'm an alien?"

THIRTY-FOUR

"So you are the hope of the Thetan race," Hank observed to Saphie as they relaxed in the yard of their Palo Alto mansion. "That's quite a lot of pressure."

"Not really; all I have to do is exist. And breed, of course," Saphie responded.

"Breed? Who do you plan on breeding with?" Hank demanded.

"With you, silly. Father is working on ways to make our DNA compatible."

"So that's what he's doing. I wondered why he needs to keep investigating my 'life center.'" Hank complained. "And, besides, when were you going to ask me if I wanted to breed?"

"Well, you do, don't you?"

"Well, yes, but…"

"But you're not sure you want an alien love child, eh? You should realize that you are lucky to have me."

"I do realize that," Hank said seriously. And he did. All his money had not brought him a fraction of the happiness he felt with Saphie. She was brilliant and sweet and he was a better man with her.

Besides, there were worse things than a girlfriend with four hands…

– AUTHOR'S FINAL NOTE

Now you know the entire story, and no doubt you appreciate my desperation. The aliens are breeding again and I don't know how to stop them.

I will continue my undercover work as a senior member of the Scientology Church in my efforts to learn more. If you see me behaving as an enthusiastic proponent of Church doctrine, do not be deceived. I must continue to play the part of a faithful member of the Church and I am a superb actor.

But I need help; I cannot do it alone. Please join my efforts, before it is too late.

BIBLIOGRAPHY

Behe, Michael J. *Darwin's Black Box: The Biochemical Challenge to Evolution*. New York: The Free Press, 1996.

Burstein, Dan, ed. *Secrets of the Code: The Unauthorized Guide to the Mysteries behind the DaVinci Code*. New York: CDS, 2004.

Chalker, Bill. *Hair of the Alien: DNA and Other Forensic Evidence of Alien Abduction*. Paraview Pocket Books, 2005.

Childress, David H. *Technology of the Gods: The Incredible Sciences of the Ancients*. Adventures Unlimited, 2000.

Colavito, Jason. *The Cult of Alien Gods: H.P. Lovecraft and Extraterrestrial Pop Culture*. Prometheus Books, 2005.

Crossan, John Dominic. *Who Killed Jesus?* New York: HarperCollins, 1995.

Demarest, R. J. *An Illustrated Guide to Human Reproduction and Fertility Control*. Taylor & Francis, 1996.

De Rosa, Peter. *Vicars of Christ: The Dark Side of the Papacy*. London: Bantam Press, 1988.

Elkington, John. *The Poisoned Womb: Human Reproduction in a Polluted World*. New York: Penguin, 1987.

Ellison, Peter T. *On Fertile Ground: A Natural History of Human Reproduction*. Harvard University Press, 2003.

Farrell, Joseph P. *The Giza Death Star Deployed: The Physics and Engineering of the Great Pyramid*. Adventures Unlimited, 2003.

Gill, Stephen, and Isabella Bakker, eds. *Power, Production and Social*

Reproduction: Human In/security in the Global Political Economy. Palgrave Macmillan, 2004.

Hancock, Graham and Robert Bauval, *Keeper of Genesis*. London: William Heinemann, 1996.

Hauerwas, Stanley, and William H. Willimon. *Where Resident Aliens Live: Exercises for Christian Practice*. Abingdon Press, 1996.

Hitching, F. *The Neck of the Giraffe*. London: Pan, 1982.

Hubbard, L. R. *Basic Scientology Picture Book*. Bridge Publications, 1985.

Hubbard, L. R. *What Is Scientology?* Bridge Publications, 1998.

Kaufman, Robert. *Inside Scientology; How I Joined Scientology and Became Superhuman*. Olympus Distributing Corporation, 1972.

Lamont, Stewart. *Religion Inc: the Church of Scientology*. Harrap, 1986.

Lehner, Mark. *The Complete Pyramids: Solving the Ancient Mysteries*. Thames & Hudson, 1997.

Lucius Apuleius. *The Golden Ass*, trans. W. Adlington. London: Harvard University Press, 1989.

MacNulty, W. K. *Freemasonry: A Journey Through Ritual and Symbol*. Thames & Hudson, 1991.

Margenau, Henry, and Roy A. Varghese, eds. *Cosmos, Bios, Theos: Scientists Reflect on Science, God, and the Origins of the Universe, Life, and Homo Sapiens*. La Salle, IL: Open Court, 1992.

Mayle, Peter. *Where Did I Come from?* Carol Publishing Corporation, 2000.

Phipps, William E. *The Sexuality of Jesus*. New York: Harper & Row, 1973.

Picknett, Lynn, and Clive Prince. *The Templar Revelation*. New York: Simon and Schuster, 1997.

Ridley, Jasper. *The Freemasons: A History of the World's Most Powerful Secret Society*. Arcade, 2002.

U.D., Frater. *Secrets of the German Sex Magicians*. St. Paul, MN: Llewellyn, 1991.

Von Daniken, Erich. *Chariots of the Gods? Unsolved Mysteries of the Past*. New York: Bantam Books, 1969.

Wilmshurst, W. L. *Meaning of Masonry*. Gramercy, 1980.

THE PUZZLES

1. When they realize the Great Pyramid is a dead end, Saphie realizes they have misinterpreted the haiku. Where does she take them?

2. Explain how Saphie managed to make the correct door choices at each of the four rooms in the alien maze. How does she know whether it is morning or afternoon?

3. What is the "true" identity of Dr. Ian Browne?

CONTEST PRIZES

The following prizes will be awarded:

One $500 gift certificate with BenBella Books
Ten $200 gift certificates with BenBella Books
Fifty $50 gift certificates with BenBella Books

Gift Certificates will be redeemable at benbellabooks.com

HOW TO ENTER

Mail your responses to:

BenBella Books
Da Vinci Mole Puzzles
6440 N. Central Expressway
Suite #617
Dallas, TX 75206

Please include your name and address.

CONTEST RULES

1. All solutions must be received by December 31, 2006. Winners will be randomly selected from respondents with correct answers. Late entries will not be considered.
2. Prizes will be awarded no later than February 15, 2007. Winners will be notified via mail. If prize notification letter or prize is returned as undeliverable, the prize will be forfeited.
3. The correctness of the responses will be judged by staff of BenBella Books, whose decisions are final.
4. No purchase necessary. Purchasing will not improve your chance of winning.
5. Limit one entry per person. Only individual persons are eligible for entry. Employees of BenBella Books are ineligible.
6. Contest subject to all federal, state and local laws and regulations. Void in Puerto Rico, the U.S. Virgin Islands, U.S. military installations in foreign countries, and where prohibited.
7. Income and other taxes, if any, on the value of the prize are the sole responsibility of the winners.

8. This contest is governed by the laws of the United States with venue in Dallas County in the State of Texas.

9. By entering, you agree to be bound by these rules. Any and all claims, judgments and awards shall be limited to actual out-of-pocket costs incurred, including costs associated with entering this promotion but in no event attorney's fees; and entrant hereby waives all rights to claim punitive, incidental, and consequential damages and any other damages, other than for actual out-of-pocket expenses, and any and all rights to have damages multiplied or otherwise increased. Some jurisdictions do not allow the limitations or exclusion of liability for incidental or consequential damages, so the above may not apply to you.

10. The contest is restricted to individuals who are of the legal age of majority in their jurisdiction of residence and are in any case at least eighteen years of age as of the date of entry in the contest.

ABOUT THE AUTHOR

DR. IAN BROWNE is the pseudonym for a well-known figure who, for reasons of security, must remain anonymous. A dashing, passionate figure, Dr. Browne has had a diverse career, including time as a jet fighter pilot, professional pool hustler, and paid assassin. He spent many years in Japan mastering the ancient art of Bushido and has been rumored to have worked for a clandestine intelligence organization. Dr. Browne has been married to two, and soon three, of the world's most beautiful women. A polymath, Dr. Browne is an expert in many fields, including the history of psychiatry. He divides his time between London and Los Angeles.